NEW DIRECTIONS FOR STUDENT SERVICES

Margaret J. Barr, *Texas Christian University*
EDITOR-IN-CHIEF

M. Lee Upcraft, *The Pennsylvania State University*
ASSOCIATE EDITOR

Crisis Intervention and Prevention

Harold L. Pruett
University of California, Los Angeles

Vivian B. Brown
PROTOTYPES

EDITORS

Number 49, Spring 1990

JOSSEY-BASS INC., PUBLISHERS
San Francisco • Oxford

Crisis Intervention and Prevention.
Harold L. Pruett, Vivian B. Brown (eds.).
New Directions for Student Services, no. 49.

NEW DIRECTIONS FOR STUDENT SERVICES
Margaret J. Barr, Editor-in-Chief
M. Lee Upcraft, Associate Editor

NEW DIRECTIONS FOR STUDENT SERVICES is part of The Jossey-Bass
Higher Education Series and is published quarterly by Jossey-Bass
Inc., Publishers (publication number USPS 449-070). Second-class
postage paid at San Francisco, California, and at additional mailing
offices. Postmaster: Send address changes to Jossey-Bass Inc.,
Publishers, 350 Sansome Street, San Francisco, California 94104.

EDITORIAL CORRESPONDENCE should be sent to the Editor-in-Chief,
Margaret J. Barr, Sadler Hall, Texas Christian University,
Fort Worth, Texas 76129.

Library of Congress Catalog Card Number LC 85-644751

International Standard Serial Number ISSN 0164-7970

International Standard Book Number ISBN 1-55542-836-3

Cover photograph by Wernher Krutein/PHOTOVAULT © 1990.

Manufactured in the United States of America. Printed on acid-free paper.

CONTENTS

Editors' Notes

Most colleges and universities are faced with providing psychological services to an increasing number of students with an increasing number of special problems—namely, drugs, alcohol, suicide, sexual assault, AIDS, and so on. Psychological and counseling services vary in models, scope, length of treatment, and modalities, but all must address the significant mental health needs of today's college and university students. One of the most promising new directions appears to be in structuring student services according to a campus-as-community mental health model that focuses on crisis intervention and prevention. With this model, the areas of concern for student services are extended to include not just individual student problems but also problems affecting the entire campus, and not just the treatment of disorders but also the enhancement of the quality of campus life.

In Chapter One, Harold L. Pruett and Vivian B. Brown present a model of intervention and prevention based on the concept of crisis. They combine their experience in community mental health centers and on campus to describe procedures for intervening in individual and community crises and developing prevention strategies. The chapter also includes examples of hands-on intervention.

Chapter Two provides an important summary of research on stress among students. Christine Dunkel-Schetter and Marci Lobel have conducted surveys of UCLA students over the past three years. Using students to survey other students, Dunkel-Schetter and Lobel present many important findings on student stress. They make recommendations for how further research in the area can be conducted to avoid problems of interpretation that have arisen with past research.

In Chapter Three, Vivian B. Brown brings her many years of experience to bear on substance abuse among college students. Using a crisis model, she describes assessment procedures, as well as intervention and prevention strategies for dealing with drug and alcohol abuse. Her case examples demonstrate the use of a crisis approach.

In Chapter Four, Harold L. Pruett discusses suicide on the college campus from a crisis perspective. He presents important components that need to be included in prevention programs, including training, dealing with administrative needs, and dealing with the community. He also offers an individual intervention strategy, using a case example, and he uses another case example to discuss postvention.

Interpersonal violence on the campus has become an increasing concern. In Chapter Five, Susan B. Sorenson and Vivian B. Brown discuss the problem of violence, including rape, sexual assault, and other forms.

New Directions for Student Services, no. 49, Spring 1990 © Jossey-Bass Inc., Publishers

They offer crucial information on crisis intervention with victims and survivors of rape and sexual assault, and they outline important components of prevention programs.

In Chapter Six, Vivian B. Brown discusses the most dramatic crisis of the century: acquired immunodeficiency syndrome (AIDS). Using the concept of the crisis matrix, she presents important information on intervention and prevention models for dealing with the AIDS crisis.

In Chapter Seven, Harold L. Pruett and Vivian B. Brown examine present and future issues confronting the counseling and mental health center. They include recommendations and offer an annotated bibliography of selected references to expand on the topics covered.

Harold L. Pruett
Vivian B. Brown
Editors

Harold L. Pruett, director of student psychological services at the University of California, Los Angeles, is also chair of the Organization of Counseling Center Directors in Higher Education in California and past president and fellow of the Los Angeles Society of Clinical Psychologists.

Vivian B. Brown is chief executive officer of PROTOTYPES, a center for innovation in health, mental health, and social services. She is also a consultant for student psychological services at the University of California, Los Angeles, and for substance abuse prevention at the California Institute of Technology.

If we are really going to meet the needs of the campus community, a crisis model should be seriously considered.

Crisis Intervention and Prevention as a Campus-as-Community Mental Health Model

Harold L. Pruett, Vivian B. Brown

Student services, especially counseling and mental health services, are facing increasingly complex and vexing problems on campuses across the country. Enhancing retention, increasing diversity, emphasizing civility, coping with the aftermath of date rape and suicide—these are only a few of the many issues that cannot be ignored.

To address the needs of students in the most effective way, services must (1) be sensitive to the increasingly diverse student population and the evolving needs of students, (2) provide services immediately, (3) take into account the vulnerabilities and special developmental issues of college students, (4) be able to respond to the entire campus environment and attempt to affect as many individuals as possible, and (5) address both treatment and prevention. One of the most successful strategies for meeting these expectations is crisis intervention.

A recent study by Rimmer, Halikas, and Schucket (1982) indicates that as many as 39 percent of all college students will experience psychological impairment at some time during their undergraduate years. This is not surprising, given the vulnerability of many college students and the difficult challenges they face. Each of the four years of college requires different tasks, and the impact of "college time" on student mental health has been described by Grayson (1985) in some detail.

The freshman entering a college or university environment must cope with many changes. For many of college age, separation is necessary from parents and other family members, high school peers, and hometown familiarity. For older students (and some of college age), separation from familiar roles and settings may be required. The student must learn to reinvest in new peers, a new community, and new authorities. In addition, the new student becomes aware of other realities: competition for grades, minimal external structure, and the need to set one's own priorities. The middle years of college are a period when the college-age student develops a more solid sense of how one interacts with others, what one's true values are, and the meaning of responsibility and commitment. In the final year of college, students begin with the process of separation all over again. As in the first year, coping with loss and transition is a vital developmental step. Such separations and discontinuities are what crises are about.

Crisis Defined

Caplan (1961, p. 18), often thought to be the father of crisis intervention, states that a crisis is provoked when "a person faces an obstacle to important life goals that are for a time insurmountable through the utilization of customary methods of problem solving. A period of disorganization ensues, a period of upset, during which many different abortive attempts at solution are made. Eventually some kind of adaptation is achieved, which may or may not be in the best interests of that person or his fellows."

It is unfortunate that the word *crisis* conjures up emergency, catastrophe, disaster. While all emergencies are crises, not all crises are emergencies. In crisis theory, the term means a *turning point,* the period of transition from one level of functioning to another, in which there may be the danger of death, disintegration, or dysfunction. At the same time, there is the opportunity for change and growth. Crisis, in the simplest terms, may be defined as an upset or a discontinuity in a person's steady state. The major elements of crisis theory have been summarized and expanded by a number of writers (Parad, 1965; Jacobson, 1980; Aguilera and Messick, 1986; Ewing, 1978), each building on the pioneering work of Lindemann (1944) and Caplan (1961).

Figure 1 describes the process of crisis and crisis intervention. The key elements are a hazardous *event, coping, time limit,* and an *outcome.*

Event. The hazardous event is similar to the concept of stressful life event. It creates for the individual a threat, a loss, or a challenge. Examples of such an event are the loss of a relationship, a serious illness, and the birth of a child. Various investigators (Jacobson, Strickler, and Morley, 1968; Rapoport, 1965) have observed that during a crisis memories of old problems that are linked symbolically to the present are stimulated and may emerge into consciousness spontaneously or can be uncovered and dealt with by relatively brief therapeutic intervention. The crisis, with its

Figure 1. Elements of a Crisis

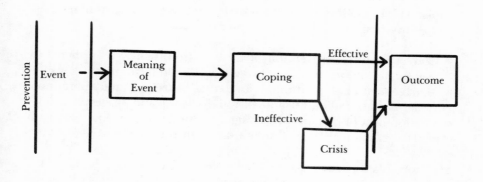

mobilization of energy, operates as a second chance to correct earlier (and faulty) problem solving. It should also be noted that a major life event often does not immediately precipitate a crisis. According to Jacobson (1980), interim coping that may be maladaptive, such as denial of bereavement, can prevent a crisis; later, however, a relatively minor occurrence (an otherwise minor rejection or loss) may invalidate this interim coping and precipitate a crisis.

The meaning given to a life event determines whether it becomes a hazard and triggers a crisis. What does this event mean to this particular individual? Some events represent universal meanings—rape, for example, which represents a threat to life, to bodily integrity, and to safety. Other events may have meaning only for the specific individual.

Coping. In crisis theory, coping involves all problem-solving strategies, including the traditional intrapsychic defense mechanisms. It is important to note that coping can be either adaptive or maladaptive. Having oneself hospitalized is a coping strategy; in many instances, however, this strategy may not be seen as highly adaptive. Abusing drugs and alcohol can be seen as coping, but in most instances it would be seen as maladaptive. In crisis work, we need to assess how the person has coped in the past and why the usual methods of coping are not working in this situation.

Outcome. An individual may resolve a crisis in one of three ways: by functioning at the same level, at a higher level, or at a lower level than before the crisis. Minimally, we wish to return the individual to his or her previous level of functioning, but we have the opportunity to effect a change to a much higher level of functioning. It is this opportunity that we do not want to miss. Crisis intervention is a method of pushing the odds toward better postcrisis functioning.

Crisis Intervention Defined

Caplan (1961) and Rapoport (1965) have outlined the patterns of response for healthy crisis resolution in the following way:

• Correct cognitive perception of the situation, which is furthered by seeking new information and by keeping the problem in consciousness
• Management of affect through awareness of feelings and appropriate verbalization, leading toward tension discharge and mastery
• Development of patterns of seeking and using interpersonal help with actual tasks and feelings, through use of institutional resources.

This formulation contains guides for crisis intervention. If there is a need for cognitive grasp and restructuring, then the first task of the intervener is to clarify the problem that has led to the call for help. Factors leading to the disruption of functioning are often preconscious and unintegrated. Kalis, Harris, Prestwood, and Freeman (1961), in their stress-precipitation studies, have shown that individuals were not fully aware of the precipitants and that prompt therapeutic focus on precipitating stressors facilitated the restoration of emotional equilibrium.

Slaiku (1984, p. 5) defines crisis intervention as a "helping process aimed at assisting a person or family to survive an unsettling event so that the probability of debilitating effects (that is, emotional scars, physical harm) is minimized, and the probability of growth (that is, new skills, new outlook on life, more options in living) is maximized."

From its earliest beginnings, in the 1940s, crisis intervention had a preventive focus. For Caplan (1964, p. 35), examination of psychiatric histories shows that "during certain of these crisis periods, the individual seems to have dealt with his problems in a maladjusted manner and to have emerged less healthy than he had been before the crisis." Danish and D'Augelli (1980, p. 61) offer an enhancement model of crisis work, where "growth is preceded by a state of imbalance or crisis which serves as the basis for future development. In fact, without crises, development is not possible."

Crisis intervention is a time-limited intervention whose goal is to restore equilibrium, assist the individual to work through the stressful event or experience, and assist the individual to gain more effective coping skills for mastering future crises. As originally formulated by Lindemann (1944) and Caplan (1964), crisis theory stressed the time-limited nature of crisis (four to six weeks). The survivors of the Coconut Grove fire in Boston showed that when resolution of grief could proceed without interruption, relief of tension came within four to six weeks after bereavement, and this period was crucial in determining whether grief would be resolved adaptively or maladaptively.

At the Benjamin Rush Center, a crisis center in Los Angeles, data gathered over two decades consistently showed that the average number of visits per person was four. At the University of California, Los Angeles (UCLA), data collected over several years indicated that between 85 and 90 percent of students who sought psychological services were seen six or fewer times. Amada (1977) reports that students at City College in San Francisco were seen for an average of fewer than three visits. Other studies of counseling-center utilization (Haggarty, Baldwin, and Liptzin, 1980; Dorosin, Gibbs, and Kaplan, 1976) report similar results. These figures reinforce the consistent findings of psychotherapy research, which indicate that even when individuals are offered longer-term therapy, they stay in treatment for an average of four to six visits.

How Is It Done?

Rapid entry is essential to crisis intervention if we are to take advantage of the client's expressed wish and heightened motivation for assistance. Thus, the student who seeks help must have immediate access, and the first session is quite important—perhaps the most important—in helping the student to stabilize. From the outset of the intervention, we attempt to communicate that we expect to accomplish our work in four to six weeks.

The first session involves the "detective work" that is so crucial to good crisis intervention. We wish to establish rapport, identify the precipitating event, understand previous coping and why it failed, and identify new coping skills and resources that may be available. We have designed a series of questions to assist interveners in moving through the first session:

1. "Why now? What brought you to the counseling center now?" (This question elicits information about the precipitating event.)

2. If the client tells you that she has been depressed for ten years, the questioning can proceed: "But you didn't seek counseling during those ten years. What made you decide to come now? Has something changed?"

3. If the client tells you that her boyfriend has just left her, then the questioning proceeds: "Can you tell me what happened? What does his leaving mean to you?" (These questions seek the meaning of the event.)

4. "Has this (or a similar loss) ever happened to you before? If so, what happened? How did you cope? What did you do?" (These questions inquire about previous coping.)

5. If the client tells you that when she lost a previous boyfriend she "got over it quickly" and found someone new immediately, questioning proceeds: "What stops you from getting over it quickly now and finding someone new?" (Why is the coping not working?)

6. If the client tells you that when she lost a previous boyfriend she became suicidal and made a suicide attempt, questioning proceeds by exploring the previous suicide attempt and assessing the potential for another suicide attempt at this time.

7. If the client tells you that she has never lost anyone before, questioning proceeds with exploration of her feelings about the current loss and her feelings of not knowing what to do in this situation.

8. Continuing the exploration of feelings, questioning focuses on helping the client to ventilate emotions that are available (sadness and guilt) and to become aware of feelings that are not readily available (anger at being abandoned): "When people lose someone important to them, they usually feel sadness, anger, and guilt. You have expressed feeling very sad and guilty. Are you feeling any anger about his leaving you?"

9. If the session has moved through these stages, the crisis intervener should be able to present a *crisis formulation* to the client. The client will indicate whether this formulation makes sense and whether it helps (Brown, 1987).

Through this process, we are able to construct a timeline with the client, identifying the events that prompted her to seek help. The timeline is often quite helpful to the client, as well as to the counselor, because it aids in making sense of seemingly incomprehensible events.

Before the end of the first session, in addition to presenting the crisis formulation, we must make an assessment of how suitable it would be to see the client as an outpatient. Suicide and homicide risks must be evaluated, as well as alcohol and drug use, misuse, and abuse. In the vast majority of cases, even when suicide and homicide risks are present, the student can be managed on an outpatient basis.

What happens in subsequent sessions? These are devoted to further clarification of the crisis, which involves dealing with its emotional aspects, bringing adaptive coping mechanisms into play (including positive social supports), and planning. If the crisis formulation has been accepted, the client can proceed to reappraise the life event and the meanings associated with it, and to make any necessary revision of inner models of herself and the world. There is relief from pressure and anxiety. Because of the emotional pain aroused by a crisis, most clients will have interrupted some aspect of the review. By the second session, the review should move on, with the help of the counselor. By the second session, the student experiences herself participating in the intervention and in her own healing.

In the fourth through sixth sessions, we reintroduce the issue of termination. This will lead to reexperience of the loss, often with a return of symptoms. It is important to remember, however, that the average number of sessions is four, and that the student will give messages that she is feeling better and is able to cope. We want to reinforce this strength. The message of crisis intervention is "You can cope, and I will be here if you need me." In crisis intervention, the student will have an opportunity to work through the termination and this loss with the counselor; this is an important step.

Case Example

C. B. is a twenty-one-year-old student in her first quarter at the university after transferring from a community college. She walks in and asks to be seen right away, as she is "extremely depressed" and "feeling suicidal." She is given an appointment at that moment. C. B. is tearful and appears agitated. In the exploration of recent events in her life that may account for her feeling so terrible, she says that there are no reasons for her to feel as bad as she does. In fact, she starts to explain all the reasons why she should not feel depressed. The therapist gently presses her, insisting that depression and suicidal feelings do not come out of the blue and must be related to things occurring in her life. The therapist then encourages her to begin to look at a timeline. As she and the therapist begin to trace the events in her life, her distress becomes more understandable to her.

C. B. lived with her parents until the recent transfer. She is quick to point out, however, that her roommate could not be better. At the time of her transfer and move, she had a fight with her best friend and has not talked to her since. She also broke up with a boyfriend at the beginning of the summer and has not dated or had any social life since transferring. The final straw is that her car broke down over the weekend, after a visit from her parents, so that she has been forced to take the bus until she can arrange to get her car fixed. In addition, during the visit with her parents, she mentioned that she was depressed and lonely, and her parents suggested that she "see someone." She panicked, thinking that she was "mentally ill" like her mother, who, C. B. says, is on lithium.

The therapist continues to point out the losses and events that have occurred over the past weeks and how C. B.'s usual coping strategies (she has generally talked to her parents and friends, getting advice and solving problems with them) have not been available to her. C. B. cries as she discusses the fight with her best friend and the breakup with her boyfriend. An evaluation is done of the suicide risk she poses; she has no plan, means, or even intent. She is encouraged to use her roommate for some needed support at this time, and she readily agrees to return the next day for a follow-up appointment.

The following day, C. B. appears much more rested and less strained. She says she has had a "wonderful" talk with her new roommate, who was very supportive and helpful, and then she had a good night's sleep. She took care of arranging for her car to be fixed, has had no problems with the bus, and is generally feeling more hopeful. Her distress is seen as something understandable, rather than as the result of a "mental illness." Other avenues open to her to feel included in the university are explored, and another follow-up appointment is scheduled for next week.

When she returns the following week, C. B. has begun to investigate other university activities in which she can participate, and she is generally feeling supported and encouraged by her very positive relationship with her roommate. She feels that she does not need to return, but she is assured that she can return in the future if she encounters any difficulties that she wants to discuss.

Developmental Tasks and the Crisis Matrix

Crisis theory also includes the idea that crises evolve from the developmental tasks of the individual's life, which have been described by Erikson (1950, 1959) and, more recently, by Havighurst (1972). Many of the students we see are moving through adolescence into young adulthood, a transition during which they must break away from family, carve out an adult role, form intimate relationships, and decide on a career path.

This period of life leads the student into a span of years during which she or he is also vulnerable to other life events, an idea that takes us to another important concept: the crisis matrix (Jacobson, 1980). The crisis matrix defines a period, extending over several months to several years, during which the individual is likely to experience a series of crises. These crises are clustered in accordance with a common guiding principle, but they have separate and unique characteristics. Thus, an individual who is experiencing a separation or a divorce will experience a number of crises along the time continuum, extending from the first discussion of separation through the remarriage of the ex-spouse. Similarly, a woman who has been sexually assaulted will experience a series of crises, beginning with the assault and moving on through reporting the attack, appearing in court, and resolving intimate relationships. Each of these crisis will be resolved in a separate way and may have an impact on future crises (see Figure 2).

Adjunctive Methods of Treatment

Psychotropic Medications. The use of psychotropic medications for students during crises is not always an easy issue to decide on. Medications can certainly be useful as adjunctive treatment for helping students who are feeling overwhelmed by anxiety or for providing important support to students who are decompensating. The judicious use of medications can sometimes make the difference between seeing a student as an outpatient and requiring his hospitalization. Before a decision to medicate is

Figure 2. Crisis Matrix

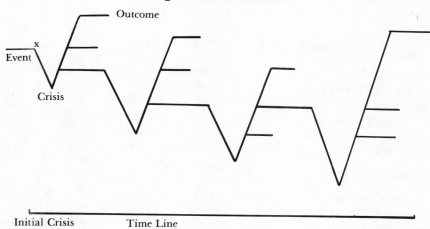

Initial Crisis   Time Line

reached, however, it is also important to consider the risks. A student may ascribe magical properties to the medication and include it in his coping repertoire in the future for any troublesome time. Medication may also threaten the student, implying that he cannot manage on his own. These and other issues should be addressed and thought out before medicating.

Crisis Groups. The group setting, while sometimes difficult for the therapist to manage, is a useful modality with the student population. Group approaches to crisis intervention have been used for a number of years at the Benjamin Rush Center, with good results (Morley and Brown, 1969; Strickler and Allgeyer, 1967). The unique advantage of a crisis group is the use of peers, to assist in discovering alternative coping and the social relationships that can grow out of the group. There are some difficulties in a crisis group, however. For example, the group has a tendency to get into discussions of chronic issues, requiring the therapist to be vigilant so that the focus remains on the crisis work. Group members may also mention coping strategies that turn out to be maladaptive for a particular client, and the therapist must be able to work these into more adaptive strategies.

The structure for crisis work in groups follows from individual intervention. One key aspect is that the first session must be an individual one. This pregroup session is the same as the first session of individual intervention. The therapist must assess the precipitating event, the hazard, and the previous and potential coping mechanisms. In addition, it is usually best to see highly suicidal or homicidal individuals in individual intervention (if they can be seen at all). After the first visit, the client enters the group and tells the other members what brought him into the center. After the nature of the students' crises has been shared, group support is encouraged, as well as exploration of coping strategies and expression of feelings.

Community Intervention

Just as in any other community, various accidents and disasters occur on the university campus, resulting in trauma to students, faculty, and staff that requires some form of management if chronic psychiatric distress is to be avoided. Like those that concern individuals, community hazards usually involve loss or threatened loss of life or property, transitions in social systems, or shifts of power. With communities, we seek to restore the population to a state of equilibrium, provide additional support to individuals who appear severely disturbed, reinforce adaptive coping strategies of the population, [and] prevent serious emotional aftermaths (Brown, 1980). Interventions on campus may also include organizational consultation, community organization, and technical assistance.

Among the losses that communities suffer, those due to disasters are the most severe. Natural disasters that may occur on a campus include fires, floods, earthquakes, and tornadoes. Man-made disasters include homicide, suicide, rape, threats of violence, and other disruptions.

In most disasters, there are two distinct phases: impact and postimpact. During the impact phase, immediate attention usually must be paid to concrete needs (shelter, food, medical attention), although emotional needs must also be addressed. Distinct interventions are usually possible after disasters (Havassy, 1987; Lawrence, 1988). First, *immediate support* is usually given right after the disaster and involves psychological help and informal crisis intervention. Second, *defusing* can occur up to forty-eight hours after an incident and usually is done in an unstructured group setting, to help people ventilate and to provide positive support, discuss coping strategies, and normalize reactions. Sometimes victims or survivors are too numb to participate, but it should not be assumed that the impact of defusing is minimal. Third, *debriefing* usually occurs from twenty-four to seventy-two hours after the incident and usually has a set format (Mitchell, 1983). The introductory phase highlights the effects of stress on functioning, normalizes people's reaction to stress, and explains the importance of debriefing. In the review phase, survivors describe where they were, what they saw, and what they did when the incident occurred. Participants contribute facts to make the incident feel real again. In the feeling phase, participants relate how they are feeling now, how they felt then, and whether they have ever felt that way before. In the symptom or reaction phase, participants relate stress responses they may be having, how their lives have changed since the incident, and any unusual experiences they are having. The facilitator normalizes reactions. In the teaching or education phase, the facilitator reviews normal stress responses and coping strategies for dealing with stress. The reentry phase is used to identify specific concerns of survivors, develop action plans for survivors, discuss any concerns about the transition back to normal routines, and discuss referrals (if and when they are needed).

Common themes of survivors' feelings after disasters are fear of repetition of the event, shame over helplessness, rage at the source, guilt over aggressive impulses, fear of loss of control, survivor guilt, and sadness in relation to loss. Debriefing should take place after any student dies on campus and after any other disaster.

In addition to the hazards already mentioned, sexual assault and rape, always a crisis for the individual, also represent the threat of disorder for the community and may require community crisis intervention. University and college communities often feel quite powerless and show fear, particularly when such hazards occur on campus and in residence halls. Rape can be seen as an ever widening crisis—moving from the individual to the floor of the residence hall to the entire residence hall to all residence halls to the whole campus. Community crisis intervention programs will involve organizing the community into support groups and community watches (see Chapter Five for further discussion).

Another hazard that is being presented in many universities and colleges across the country involves the changing ethnic and racial composition of the student population. Such change is often accompanied by hostility, fear, and misunderstanding (Brown, 1976). Crisis intervention in such instances may involve the development of committees, or of a task force made up of community representatives (faculty, staff, students) and other resource persons, in order to deescalate the hostilities, facilitate communication, and develop a program to allow for some equitable distribution of power.

Prevention

Crisis theory also leads us into the area of prevention (Caplan, 1964). If we can identify and define stressful life events, and if we can describe typical processes of coping with these events, then we should be able to implement prevention programs. (Crisis intervention itself can be seen as a secondary prevention strategy, since it prevents more serious emotional disorders by providing immediate attention.) When we look at such phenomena as rape, substance abuse, AIDS, and suicide, we wish to prevent them. If we cannot, then our goal becomes to build strength in coping, in order to help people withstand more disastrous consequences. Four principles of prevention can be derived from crisis work (Jacobson and Brown, 1982):

1. Work with key persons, including caregivers
2. Work with populations at risk

3. Train people in coping skills
4. Work with social networks.

Work with Key Persons. Preparedness is extremely important; it allows a set of procedures to be developed, so that the response to a disaster can be orderly and effective. Ideally, a disaster plan should not only delineate roles for various campus offices but also involve predisaster training (fire drills, earthquake drills) for community members, so that dangers and coping strategies can be understood and rehearsed. Key persons include health care providers, security personnel and police, faculty, advisers, student affairs personnel, and coaches.

Work with Populations at Risk. Some of the populations that may be at risk for emotional disturbance are incoming students who are from countries undergoing war, violence, or political upheaval; students who experience the death of a parent; and students from dysfunctional families. The importance of identifying such at-risk groups lies in the possibility of establishing specialized group programs to prevent serious disorders. In the case of students from countries that are undergoing major upheaval and violence, it is important to understand posttraumatic stress issues within a cultural context. For example, with students from Vietnam, counselors may not wish to encourage reliving of the trauma.

Training People in Coping Skills. Certain life events may be quite disturbing because the student does not have the coping skills to reduce distress. Death of a loved one and bereavement can distress many students, particularly if they are far away from home and have never before experienced such a loss. Preventive education allows the student to learn what grief is, what normal feelings of grief are, what actions may help, how long he may experience the feelings and thoughts, and so on. Other areas for preventive education are first dating experiences, first sexual experiences, cross-cultural education, conflict resolution, and coping with role transitions (particularly with reentering students).

Work with Social Networks. It is extremely important to work with peers and support systems on campus. These may include residence halls, fraternities and sororities, religious groups, athletic teams, and student organizations. These are the natural support networks for students and may be keys to prevention work for such events as suicide. We have also been concerned with providing additional support during times of stress or crisis. If the hazardous event is, for example, the suicide of a student in a fraternity, it affects the immediate support system directly and can therefore affect the support group members' ability to help one another. In this case, it may be important to have another social system, which is not directly involved, help in providing support.

Summary

One of the most successful strategies for dealing with individual and campus issues is crisis intervention. Crisis intervention is a model for both intervention and prevention and offers guidelines that are both practical and relevant to emerging institutional needs. A *crisis* can be defined as an upset or discontinuity in an individual's, a community's, or an institution's functioning.

Key elements of crisis intervention include a hazardous event, coping, and an outcome. The goal of crisis intervention is to help the individual or institution work through the stressful event and gain more effective coping skills for mastering future crises.

References

Aguilera, D. C., and Messick, J. M. *Crisis Intervention: Theory and Methodology.* St. Louis: Mosby, 1986.

Amada, G. "Crisis-Oriented Psychotherapy: Some Theoretical and Practical Considerations." *Journal of Contemporary Psychotherapy,* 1977, *9,* 104–114.

Brown, V. B. "Community Crisis Intervention: The Dangers and Opportunities for Change." In H. J. Parad, H.L.P. Resnik, and L. Parad (eds.), *Emergency and Disaster Management.* Bowie, Md.: Charles Press, 1976.

Brown, V. B. "The Community in Crisis." In G. F. Jacobson (ed.), *Crisis Intervention in the 1980s.* New Directions for Mental Health Services, no. 6. San Francisco: Jossey-Bass, 1980.

Brown, V. B. "Crisis Intervention." Paper presented at University of California training conference, Los Angeles, 1987.

Caplan, G. *An Approach to Community Mental Health.* New York: Grune & Stratton, 1961.

Caplan, G. *Principles of Preventive Psychiatry.* New York: Basic Books, 1964.

Danish, S. J., and D'Augelli, A. R. "Promoting Competence and Enhancing Development Through Life Development Intervention." In L. A. Bond and J. C. Rosen (eds.), *Competence and Coping During Adulthood.* Hanover, N. H.: University Press of New England, 1980.

Dorosin, D., Gibbs, J., and Kaplan, L. "Very Brief Interventions—A Pilot Evaluation." *Journal of the American College Health Association,* 1976, *24,* 191–194.

Erikson, E. H. *Childhood and Society.* New York: Norton, 1950.

Erikson, E. H. *Identity and the Life Cycle.* New York: International Universities Press, 1959.

Ewing, C. P. *Crisis Intervention as Psychotherapy.* New York: Oxford University Press, 1978.

Grayson, P. A. "College Time: Implications for Student Mental Health Services." *Journal of the American College Health Association,* 1985, *33,* 198–204.

Haggarty, J. J., Jr., Baldwin, B. A., and Liptzin, M. B. "Very Brief Interventions in College Mental Health." *Journal of the American College Health Association,* 1980, *28,* 326–329.

Havassy, V. J. "Rescue Workers as Victims." Paper presented at the World Congress on Victimology, San Francisco, July 1987.

Havighurst, R. J. *Developmental Tasks and Education*. (3rd ed.) New York: McKay, 1972.

Jacobson, G. F. (ed.). *Crisis Intervention in the 1980s*. New Directions for Mental Health Services, no. 6. San Francisco: Jossey-Bass, 1980.

Jacobson, G. F., and Brown, V. B. "Community Mental Health Centers as Sites for Prevention Programs and Research: An Example." In R. L. Hough, P. A. Gongla, V. B. Brown, and S. E. Goldston (eds.), *Psychiatric Epidemiology and Prevention: The Possibilities*. Los Angeles: Neuropsychiatric Institute, University of California, 1982.

Jacobson, G. F., Strickler, M., and Morley, W. E. "Generic and Individual Approaches to Crisis Intervention." *American Journal of Public Health*, 1968, *58* (2), 338–343.

Kalis, L., Harris, M. R., Prestwood, A. R., and Freeman, E. H. "Precipitating Stress as a Focus in Psychotherapy." *Archives of General Psychiatry*, 1961, *5*, 219–228.

Lawrence, C. "Managing Trauma After Disaster Occurs: A Focused Intervention Model." Paper presented to the International Association of Airline Employee Assistance Programs, May 1988.

Lindemann, E. "Symptomatology and Management of Acute Grief." *American Journal of Psychiatry*, 1944, *101*, 141–148.

Mitchell, J. T. "When Disaster Strikes . . . The Critical Incident Debriefing Process." *Journal of Emergency Medical Services*, 1983, *8*, 36–39.

Morley, W. E., and Brown, V. B. "The Crisis Intervention Group: A Natural Mating or a Marriage of Convenience?" *Psychotherapy*, 1969, *6*, 30–36.

Parad, H. J. (ed.). *Crisis Intervention: Selected Readings*. New York: Family Service Association of America, 1965.

Rapoport, L. "The State of Crisis: Some Theoretical Considerations." In H. J. Parad (ed.), *Crisis Intervention: Selected Readings*. New York: Family Service Association of America, 1965.

Rimmer, J., Halikas, J. A., and Schucket, M. A. "Prevalence and Incidence of Psychiatric Illness in College Students: A Four-Year Prospective Study." *Journal of the American College Health Association*, 1982, *30*, 207–211.

Slaiku, K. A. *Crisis Intervention: A Handbook for Practice and Research*. Newton, Mass.: Allyn & Bacon, 1984.

Strickler, M., and Allgeyer, J. "The Crisis Group: A New Application of Crisis Theory." *Social Casework*, 1967, *12*, 28–32.

Harold L. Pruett, director of student psychological services at the University of California, Los Angeles, is also chair of the Organization of Counseling Center Directors in Higher Education in California and past president and fellow of the Los Angeles Society of Clinical Psychologists.

Vivian B. Brown is chief executive officer of PROTOTYPES, a center for innovation in health, mental health, and social services. She is also a consultant for student psychological services at the University of California, Los Angeles, and for substance abuse prevention at the California Institute of Technology.

College students today experience high levels of stress in many areas of life. This is an important realm for further research and a potent avenue of intervention for college mental health professionals.

Stress Among Students

Christine Dunkel-Schetter, Marci Lobel

> My most remembered stressful experience deals with my first year here . . . finals week of my first quarter. I had never encountered such heavy stress for that long a period in my life. Not only was this finals week stressful to me, it was stressful to the whole dorm I lived in. The majority of the people in the dorm were living, breathing stress machines.
>
> —Personal Communication

Stress is ubiquitous, not only in American society but around the world (Antonovsky, 1979). To most of us, this is not news. What is sometimes surprising, however, is that college students in the United States today experience high levels of stress: "College age youth are thought by the general public to be engaged in a perpetual round of adventure and merriment and to be somehow immune from mundane cares and concerns of establishing an identity and dealing with the unexpected" (La-Grand, 1985, p. 15). In fact, the college years are quite stressful, and the effects of stress are further cause for concern. Stress has various negative consequences for physical health (Cebelin and Hirsch, 1980; DeLongis and others, 1982; Jemmott and Locke, 1984) and mental health (Grant, Sweetwood, Yager, and Gerst, 1978; Kanner, Coyne, Schaeffer, and Lazarus, 1981; Surtees and Ingham, 1980). For college students in particular, stress may be a contributor to the high incidence in this population of depression and suicide, substance abuse, such eating disorders as bulimia and anorexia nervosa, and poor academic performance and attrition from college. This chapter addresses stress in college students by bringing together past research with research we have conducted at UCLA. The goals of the chapter are to highlight the nature and extent of students' stressful experiences and to delineate some of the major conceptual and methodological issues involved in studying this topic.

Past Research on Stress Among College Students

Stress-Related Research with Students. Several bodies of research are relevant to the topic of stress in students, but most studies have not focused on the actual stressful experiences of the full spectrum of students. Past research has often concentrated on various behavioral problems that are causes for seeking help from campus mental health centers. Clusters of studies have investigated depression (Sherer, 1985), psychiatric disturbance (Reifler, 1971; Thompson, Bentz, and Liptzin, 1973), eating disorders (Pyle, Halvorson, Neuman, and Mitchell, 1986), drug abuse (Stokes, 1974), alcoholism (Brennan, Walfish, and AuBuchon, 1986), and suicide (Bernard and Bernard, 1985) on campus. Research of this sort is usually on the incidence of diagnosable disorders and on treatment. The causes of these disorders among students may lie outside the institution, yet there is reason to believe that high levels of stress among students may contribute to the high prevalence of these problems on campus.

A smaller body of related research links stressful life events with poor physical and mental health (Kessler, Price, and Wortman, 1985). As in the research on adults, major negative life events, such as the death of a loved one, have been associated with various symptoms or illnesses in students, including high blood pressure (Myers, Bastien, and Miles, 1983) and affective disorders (Ionescu and Popescu, 1986). Stronger links are typically found when social support or other resources are not available to buffer the effects of these stressful life events (Cohen and Hoberman, 1983).

Another focus of past research is on adjustment to college in entering students (for example, Compas, Wagner, Slavin, and Vannatta, 1986; Cutrona, 1982). The first year of college is often a difficult one: students leave support systems and form new friendships; there are high and often unclear academic demands and a large number of new distractions (Lecompte, 1986). A related portion of past research examines concerns, stress, and adjustment in particular subgroups—for example, ethnic minority students (Gunnings, 1982; Edmunds, 1984; Fleming, 1981; Pliner and Brown, 1985). Research on entering college students and on particular subgroups of students can pinpoint high-risk groups, but it may overlook a high incidence of stress in the remaining portion of the student body.

Prevalence of Stress and Distress on Campus. In the 1970s, a cluster of studies appeared on the high prevalence of emotional distress among college students in general. For example, Comstock and Slome (1973) surveyed a random sample of 1,260 university students in North Carolina and found that 30 percent had moderate to severe emotional problems. Similarly, a standard psychiatric assessment showed high levels of distress among a random sample of 1,502 students in a large public university in the Midwest (Mechanic and Greenley, 1976). Moos and Van Dort (1977) reported that 25 to 75 percent of nearly 1,300 freshmen from two contrasting university campuses complained of emotional symptoms at some time during their first year. Finally, Christenfeld and Black (1977), using the Spielberger State Anxiety Inventory, found strikingly high mood disturbance (anxiety and depression) in 214 undergraduates at a small, liberal arts college.

Apparently, stress in college students has increased in the 1980s (Astin and others, 1988; Koplik and DeVito, 1986). In 1983, *Newsweek on Campus* reported that 59 percent of over 500 students in the magazine's national poll suffered stress, burnout, depression, or anxiety during college ("The Stress Syndrome . . . ," 1983). Four years later ("The Perils of Burnout," 1987), the magazine reported that "stress is running even higher than usual at colleges this fall." A survey of undergraduate males at a midwestern university found 93 percent had experienced physical signs of stress, such as headaches, and 88 percent had experienced stress-related feelings, such as depression (Pinch, Heck, and Vinal, 1986).

In summary, although the number of studies examining stress among college students is not large, the available research indicates that a student's college or university life today does not reflect the classic image of a blissful late adolescence within the ivory tower, where the strains of the real world are nonexistent. Instead, the picture is one of a troubled and difficult time, the sources of which are only somewhat understood.

Sources of Stress on Campus. A few studies have addressed different sources of stress for students, although this is rarely the main focus of the research. For example, more than 7,000 undergraduates randomly sampled from thirty-four New England colleges and universities completed a mail questionnaire that included questions about twenty-one common concerns and feelings of college students (Wechsler, Rohman, and Solomon, 1981). Nearly one-third of the students reported at least one anxiety-related concern; 23 percent reported difficulties with interpersonal relationships, 20 percent reported motivational problems associated with depression, and 14 percent reported that being depressed had been a major problem for them in the past year.

In another study, 265 students completed questionnaires at a medium-size university in Virginia (Beard, Elmore, and Lange, 1982). Twenty types of potential stress were covered within three areas: personal-social, vocational, and academic. The most common stressful areas for students were academic concerns, sexuality, and interpersonal relationships.

In a third investigation, Zitzow (1984) developed an instrument to assess student life events and their intensity with 1,146 students from four colleges in different regions of the country. Academic, social, personal, and family-home events were included in questionnaires. The six top-rated sources of stress were all of an academic nature, including self-induced pressure to get good grades (96 percent) and studying for tests (96 percent). Other frequent sources of stress included concern over problems of friends (84 percent), depression (82 percent), lack of self-confidence (78 percent), difficulty in budgeting money (82 percent), and anxiety or tension (79 percent).

Pinch, Heck, and Vinal (1986) also addressed these issues in a study of 313 male freshmen who were dorm residents in a midwestern university. The students completed a long questionnaire on health issues that included information on stress. School workload (88 percent) and finances (59 percent) were identified as major contributors to stress.

Finally, LaGrand (1985) asked over 3,000 students to indicate their most recent major loss: 28 percent had recently experienced the death of a loved one, and 25 percent had experienced the breakup of a love relationship. LaGrand concludes that grieving is extremely common among college students, although it often goes unnoticed and untreated.

To summarize, the primary sources of stress identified in past studies appear to be academic demands, interpersonal issues, financial concerns, and sexuality. In addition, it appears that emotional distress stemming from any cause is itself a source of stress.

UCLA Stress Surveys

In a series of surveys over three years, we attempted to explore the dimensions and extent of stress felt by undergraduates at our institution, UCLA. Surveys were conducted in 1983, 1984, and 1985 as part of an undergraduate course in survey research methods that contained approximately ten senior psychology majors. Each year, 150 to 180 male and female students were interviewed by the class. The characteristics of these three samples appear in Table 1.

The content of the surveys varied somewhat over the three years, as a function of the particular research interests of the students conducting the study. In 1983, the survey was on general stress. In 1984, it focused on health habits. The 1985 survey dealt with coping strategies used to manage stress. The descriptive profile of stress reported here was only one of several goals of the class surveys.

Characteristics of the University. UCLA is a large public university in an urban setting. It enrolls over 20,000 undergraduates per year. The student body is extremely diverse in terms of social class, ethnicity, and age; most students (92 percent) are from California. Approximately 24 percent live at home and commute, 53 percent live in off-campus hous-

Table 1. Sample and Population Characteristics

	1983	1984	1985	UCLA
Sample size	161	187	150	
Male	45%	50%	33%	49%
Female	55%	50%	67%	51%
White	65%	63%	60%	61%
Asian		20%	22%	22%
Hispanic	35%	6%	10%	9%
Black		5%	5%	6%
Other		6%	4%	2%
Freshman	24%	24%	14%	28%
Sophomore	20%	23%	15%	21%
Junior	34%	31%	25%	29%
Senior	21%	22%	45%	14%
Average age	21	21	22	21
Age range	17–66	17–48	16–46	—
Employed	71%	54%	60%	—
Average hrs/wk	18	16	—	—
Range hrs/wk	2-55	3-60	—	—
From California	82%	—	—	92%[a]
From Los Angeles	62%	—	—	—
Average GPA	3.1	—	—	3.78[a]

[a]Figures for fall 1988

ing, and 23 percent live on campus in residence halls, fraternities, or sororities.

Sampling. For our surveys, a random sample of all currently enrolled undergraduates was requested each year from the university registrar during the fall quarter. Students' names, addresses, telephone numbers, and years in school were provided to the instructor. Interviewers were given only the telephone numbers and first names of students.

Computer-Assisted Telephone Interviewing. The surveys were conducted by telephone, with a computer-assisted telephone interviewing (CATI) system (Shure and Meeker, 1978). In this system, the interview is conducted at a computer terminal, where the interviewer's questions appear on the monitor, and respondents' answers are entered immediately via the keyboard. The data are then automatically coded and can easily be compiled to obtain rapid results when the survey has been completed.

Procedures and Response Rates. Interviews were conducted in the evenings and on weekends because students had classes or other commitments on weekdays. Data collection was halted after two weeks, to allow students in the class to conduct data analyses and write research reports within the limits of the ten-week quarter. Approximately 50 percent of the sampled students were contacted each year, and these students agreed to be interviewed (40 percent of the students sampled were either not home when called or no longer reachable by phone, and refusal rates averaged about 10 percent).

Ideally, a telephone survey such as this one would obtain a 65 percent or better response rate, but our refusal rate was still lower than usual (Fowler, 1984). Moreover, comparison of the sampled students' characteristics to those of the entire student body indicates that our samples were quite similar in composition to the student body as a whole with respect to gender, race, age, and year in school. The low refusal rates also suggest that if the studies had been continued over longer periods of time, and if calls had been placed during the day, a higher response rate would probably have been obtained. The main source of bias is likely to be overrepresentation of students who are at home evenings and weekends and underrepresentation of those students who happened not to be at home when they were called.

Measures. The interview each year consisted of a specific set of questions, developed and pretested by the class, that took approximately ten to fifteen minutes to administer. Questions were included on a variety of potentially stressful domains, such as social life, academics, family, and finances. Virtually all of the questions had structured-response alternatives involving a four- or five-point scale (*never, rarely, sometimes, often,* or *very often*). Whenever possible, standard questions were taken from inventories that had been previously validated, such as the Perceived Stress Scale (Cohen, Karmarck, and Mermelstein, 1983) and the CES-D (Radloff, 1977). However, brief questions on the topics of interest were often not available and had to be devised. Some of the items on academic stress, interpersonal stress, financial stress, and perceived stress were used in more than one year.

Profile of Undergraduate Stress

General Levels of Stress. Over the three years of this set of surveys, one-third to one-half of the samples said they often or very often experienced stress as students. In our first survey, 30 to 60 percent (depending on the way the question was worded) reported having shown signs of depression during the preceding month. In the second survey, 15 percent reported that they had been depressed often or fairly often in the preceding month; 8 percent also said they "couldn't shake the blues" during that time. Two-thirds reported current problems with eating and sleeping or with illness.

Academic Stress. High levels of academic stress were reported by between one- and two-thirds of the samples over the three years. In 1983, 65 percent of the students said competition was stressful for them, and 83 percent said they felt that how well they did academically was "uncontrollable." Further, 71 percent said they were anxious about tests, and 78 percent felt time pressure. As might be expected, students who felt the most academic stress were also those who reported a greater need to achieve in college. Two years later, we tried to narrow the questions down, in order to identify the number of students who were under extreme academic pressure. We found 31 percent who reported that they were "usually overwhelmed by course work," and 20 percent said that grade-point average was a "constant worry" for them.

Stress in Family Relationships. The family appeared to be a major source of stress for many students. More than one-third of the students sampled in each of the first two years felt burdened by family responsibilities, had trouble relating to their parents, and said their families were currently having difficulties. In the first survey, 75 percent of the students reported having conflicts with their parents two times a week or more, and 85 percent said they did not get along with their parents.

Although the family was clearly a source of stress for many students, it was also a source of social support. For example, in the second survey, 85 percent of the students said their families were somewhat or very supportive. This pattern fits well with past research in which the double-edged nature of social relationships has been discussed (Abbey, Abramis, and Caplan, 1985; Rook, 1984; Wortman and Dunkel-Schetter, 1987).

Stress in Social Relationships. Results from all three surveys indicate that students have considerable difficulty forming and maintaining social relationships with their peers. About one-half of the sample for the first survey had no romantic relationships. One-third said it was difficult to start romantic relationships, and 60 percent said it was difficult to keep them. In addition, 27 percent said it was difficult to make friends, and 14 percent were lonely often or very often. In the second and third surveys, similar or larger numbers of students said it was difficult to make friends (27 percent, 65 percent) and to form romantic relationships (48 percent, 55 percent). We also found in 1983 that 44 percent did not socialize frequently with fellow students; half of this group rarely or never did. More than 50 percent of the sample did not belong to any social groups on campus, 11 percent had no friends on campus, and another 6 percent reported having only one friend.

Despite this picture, there is again evidence of the two-sided nature of relationships. In 1983, 90 percent of the sample reported receiving each of five different types of support from someone (love/caring, understanding, someone to listen, advice/information, small favor). Providers of support were usually friends; rarely were they parents or someone affiliated with the university. Low use of formal university sources of support were also evident in that only 9 percent of the sample had ever confided in a professional campus counselor and only 11 percent in a peer counselor.

Financial Stress. In the first two surveys, we asked about financial strain and found considerable evidence of its existence among students. In the first year, 57 percent felt it was a burden to pay tuition and living expenses. The next year, 40 percent said financial responsibilities were "overwhelming often or very often." In addition, we learned that two-thirds of the students interviewed were employed, and the average number of hours worked was seventeen per week (with a range of from two to sixty hours).

Consequences or Correlates of Stress in College. Simple correlational analyses indicated that some of our variables were interrelated significantly in meaningful patterns ($p < .05$). Feeling academically stressed as a student was associated with feeling significantly less good about oneself and about one's life. Experiencing family stress or financial stress was associated significantly with being depressed and feeling more overwhelmed by stress in one's life in general. Participating in activities with other students was inversely related to depression and positively associated with feeling healthy and physically fit (see Reifman and Dunkel-Schetter, in press, for details). Furthermore, belonging to social groups, having more friends on campus and socializing with students were all associated with significantly greater satisfaction in college. In turn, lower satisfaction with the campus was associated with having attended a high school that was dissimilar to the university.

Effects of Gender, Ethnicity, and Year in College. Women reported significantly higher levels of stress than men in two out of the three surveys we are discussing here. Women also sought and received more support. In general, female students reported coping with stressful situations in different ways than male students reported. Women were more likely than men to say they appraised a situation as controllable, sought support, confronted a problem, and solved a problem. Men, in contrast, were more likely to say they used less active forms of coping with stress, such as self-control and positive reappraisal.

No stable differences emerged among ethnic groups in analyses of the variables studied, although the number of black and Hispanic students in the samples was not sufficiently large for statistically powerful tests. There were also no clear patterns of difference among freshmen, sophomores, juniors, and seniors, possibly because of the great age diversity of students on this campus.

Implications and Conclusions

Two conclusions, and several inferences, can be drawn from our review of the literature and our research on stress in college students. First, it is quite clear that college students are not immune to stress, nor are they necessarily protected from the sorts of stress that occur in the general population. Students experience what appear to be high levels of stress in several domains of life, which simultaneously include their friendships and romantic relationships, family relationships, financial affairs, and academic work. In fact, because many students have not experienced such high levels of stress before, they may lack insight or skills for coping with it.

Many students in our surveys worked full-time while also taking a full-time course load. Because of the rising cost of college, together with declines in federal aid, students are carrying more of the financial burden themselves through jobs and loans, and they are relying on their parents more (Astin and others, 1988; "The Perils of Burnout," 1987). If families provide substantial support, students may worry about the burden their families bear. Academic pressure can be exacerbated when the financial and personal costs of an education are so high. Students are likely to feel that it is essential to excel in order to justify the major sacrifices they are making.

The general public, as well as academic personnel at all levels, must therefore recognize that college students are psychologically vulnerable. Furthermore, institutions of higher learning may need to be especially responsive to this fact. It may be harder to learn under circumstances of high stress than under lower levels of stress. Extremely high levels of stress can impair concentration and problem solving, as well as disrupt emotional stability (Gatchel, Baum, and Krantz, 1989). Overburdened schedules lead students to gear studying to test performance, rather than to retention over time. Stress can also make it difficult to manage time effectively and meet course-work deadlines.

The second conclusion we can draw is that these issues merit much more systematic investigation. Sufficient preliminary research exists to highlight the potential importance of stress on campus, yet without methodologically sophisticated and up-to-date research the issues cannot be fully comprehended or responded to by colleges and universities. Carefully designed, national studies must be the next step in determining the full extent and nature of stress for college students.

Methodological Considerations in Student Stress Research. Several features of the way our surveys were conducted merit emphasis. First, CATI is an excellent resource for college officials who wish to examine these or other issues in a rigorous, inexpensive, and expedient fashion. Telephone interviews are practical because they are not as expensive or time-consuming as face-to-face interviews, yet they are much easier for student respondents than completing a questionnaire, and they have higher response rates than mail questionnaires (Frey, 1983).

Second, the use of student interviewers is valuable for increasing the quality of the data, at least on larger campuses, where interviews can be conducted without violating students' privacy. We found that students were uniquely well qualified to conduct interviews because of their status as peers, which seemed to decrease rates of refusal over the rates usually achieved in telephone surveys and contributed to good rapport and honesty during interviews.

A third feature was the use of the registrar's computerized student records to obtain a random sample of students. The importance of a representative sample in student surveys is paramount because the goal is to obtain an accurate picture of the experiences of the student body as a whole. Sampling in any nonrandom manner will potentially bias results and undermine their value. It is also possible through computerized records to sample for equal numbers of specific groups, such as equal numbers of men and women, equal numbers of students across classes, or equal numbers of students from various ethnic groups, in order to permit comparisons of subgroups.

The development of standard measures of student stress that can be used across campuses is also highly desirable. This would permit comparison of different campus environments, as well as comparisons from year to year. Standard measures have rarely been used in past research on stress with college students, partly because they are usually long and cannot be included in brief surveys. Researchers may need to devote considerable time to pilot-testing, in order to develop a brief but reliable and valid set of survey questions before adopting a standard set, but the benefits of this process are clear.

It is notable that each of our surveys was cross-sectional, involving the collection of data at only one point in time, a procedure that does not permit inferences about causes and effects. For example, we found that academically stressed students felt less good about themselves and their lives, but we cannot tell whether this means that academic stress causes decrements in self-esteem and life satisfaction or whether it means that students low in self-esteem and life satisfaction tend to experience more academic stress. The only way to untangle these possibilities is to collect data from a particular sample of students over time. Longitudinal or panel survey designs—beginning, ideally, with precollege baseline data—will yield the most accurate and complete information about causes and consequences of stress in students. This type of research is very much needed.

Conceptualizations of Stress and Their Applicability to Students. Past research on stress in college students is generally atheoretical and uninformed by the vast body of theory and research on life stress, yet the use of theoretical definitions and frameworks can aid in formulating the problems to study among college students, the methods of study, and the framing of conclusions. For example, past research with college students has not generally used explicit definitions of the term *stress*. Unless the term is defined, there may be disagreement about what the basic phenomenon is. To stress researchers, stress is not synonymous with depression and anxiety, although the term is often used in this way by those outside the field.

Historically, stress has been conceptualized as either a stimulus (an event occurring in the external environment) or as a response (an emotional or physiological reaction (Lazarus and Folkman, 1984; Hobfoll, 1989). Most current definitions are more complex than this, however, incorporating environmental events, perceptions of them by the individual, and a variety of possible levels of response (Hobfoll, 1989).

The most widely accepted conceptualization of stress at present is probably that of Lazarus and his colleagues (Lazarus, 1966; Lazarus and Launier, 1978; Lazarus and Folkman, 1984). This work has served as the basis for defining variables and examining their interrelationships in our research on student stress. *Psychological stress* is defined as a particular relationship between the person and the environment that is appraised by the person as taxing or exceeding his or her resources and endangering his or her well-being (Lazarus and Folkman, 1984). This definition has several key components. First, stress involves transactions between the person and the environment that are rapidly changing. Second, the emphasis is on how a person perceives a situation (that is, as threatening or challenging), rather than on objective aspects of the situation. Third, a situation is perceived as stressful when the ability to manage it exceeds ordinary adaptive capabilities.

Lazarus and Folkman (1984) also distinguish among the antecedents of stress, the mediating stress and coping process, and the consequences of stress for adaptation. The term *antecedents* refers to aspects of oneself or the environment that make one vulnerable or resistant to stress, such as one's values, commitments, and beliefs and one's social network, genetic predisposition, or material resources. The *stress process* includes cognitive appraisal (or how one perceives a stressful situation) and coping responses, which are cognitive and behavioral strategies to manage stress. *Stress consequences* include physiological changes, emotions, morale, and social functioning, which may be grouped according to immediate or longer-term effects.

This framework for conceptualizing stress has good applicability to college student populations because students are experiencing stress partly as a function of the campus environment and partly as a function of their own inexperience, lack of skills, or other personal vulnerabilities. By emphasizing both the environmental component of stress and the person's contribution, this definition explains why almost all students have trouble adjusting during the first year of college, why some students have more trouble than others, and why a few do not ever successfully adjust to college. Research that considers environmental factors that increase the prevalence of student stress, as well as dispositional factors that increase students' vulnerability to stressful college environments, could be especially valuable (Tracey, Sherry, and Keitel, 1986).

Acute and Chronic Forms of Stress. One simple and potentially useful distinction between different forms of stress is the distinction between acute and chronic stress. *Acute stress* refers to the experience of discrete events of limited duration, varying in intensity from slight (for example, daily irritants or "hassles," such as a flat tire or long course-registration lines) to fairly strong (for example, major life events, such as personal injury or the sudden death of a close relative). Jacobson's (1974, 1979) reviews of crisis theory suggest that what is often called a *crisis* in psychiatry and community or counseling psychology is similar to what we refer to here as *strong acute stress; crisis* is defined as an acute stage lasting no longer than four to six weeks, with a specific date of onset (Jacobson, 1974, 1979). *Chronic stress*, by contrast, is of longer duration and often involves a gradual onset. Its causes include widespread conditions (for example, economic recession, war), as well as individualized chronic conditions (for example, financial difficulties, job strain, caring for an infant).

Both acute and chronic stress are experienced by undergraduate students in university and college settings. For a number of years, we asked undergraduates in a health psychology class at our university to describe the most stressful situations they had experienced in the preceding month. In a class of thirty undergraduates, no one had difficulty describing a stressful experience, and very few of these were of a minor nature. In all, about half reported an acute stressor during the preceding month, and half reported some form of chronic stress. Acute stressors included hospitalization for substance abuse, sexual assault, death of a parent by suicide, a serious knee injury, sudden marital and relationship breakups, car accidents, and loss of a job. Among the chronic stressors were relationship tension with parents or partners, physical separation from loved ones, work pressure, time pressure, academic pressure, difficult adjustments after moving, and difficult career or personal decisions.

Because of the treatment implications of these two different forms of stress, it may be useful in future research to distinguish them and to examine their prevalence. College mental health services must often focus on acute stress because it precipitates help-seeking behavior. However, the chronic stress experienced by students today is also worthy of attention. Most of the stress-related questions in our surveys concerned chronic stress, and we found notably high levels of chronic stress in the family, peer, academic, and financial domains of students' lives. Chronic stress is actually the context within which acute stressors occur. If a student's personal resources (such as health and energy, finances, coping skills, or interpersonal relationships) are already taxed by chronic stress, then the occurrence of an acute event, even one of small magnitude, may have the potential to trigger a crisis.

Policy Implications. The themes developed in this chapter have many policy implications. These can be divided into three types: methods for increasing awareness of student stress, prevention programs, and intervention methods directed toward students experiencing stress. Few of the following suggestions for policymakers are novel; many institutions now have them in place.

Where methods to increase awareness are concerned, there should be multiple benefits for students, parents, faculty, and administrators. The recognition that stress is prevalent in college can help students to have more realistic expectations for their own experience and less likelihood of feeling inadequate or abnormal if they become overwhelmed by extreme demands at any point. For parents, faculty, and administrators, awareness may lead to increased supportiveness and sensitivity. Among faculty members, greater awareness of the high levels of personal stress that students often shoulder could be helpful in planning course work that is realistically geared to students' abilities. Awareness on the part of administrators should lead to the devoting of more resources aimed at reducing stress among students and enhancing their opportunities for learning under conditions of stress.

There are a number of ways to increase awareness of the prevalence and sources of stress on campus. Factual brochures can be developed for students and parents and distributed at the time of enrollment. Workshops, panels, or lectures concerning stress in college could be incorporated into new-student orientation and developed as special campus events; many medical schools already have such programs, which could serve as models. Another possibility would be to publish a quarterly newsletter on campus health, aimed toward increasing community well-being. It could include brief summaries of recent research on college students' health, information on physical health and mental health in general, and periodic updates on campus programs for students. Besides having practical benefits, such a newsletter could function both as a regular reminder that stress is common among students and as a source of information on how stress can be managed effectively. The newsletter could also be sent to parents, faculty, and administrators. Related ideas could be to submit a series of articles on stress in college to the school newspaper, or to disseminate information through the campus radio station. Finally, videotapes can be produced about sources of stress on campus and effective ways to cope with stress. These could be checked out by students and used in student orientation or mental health programs.

With respect to primary prevention, increasing the availability and amount of financial aid would undoubtedly reduce the burden on students who now work for pay more than twenty hours per week. Another improvement would be to structure course requirements and curriculum requirements. Course work usually requires students to meet many deadlines within a short quarter or semester. Students who have other roles besides that of student (such as parent or employee) often have difficulty meeting rigid deadlines, but they may be able to meet course requirements if courses are structured somewhat flexibly. For example, rather than administering five required quizzes, an instructor could allow students to take any five of six quizzes and miss one of their own choosing. To meet college major requirements, students could be allowed some degree of self-determination over setting deadlines for completion of specific steps, perhaps by developing contracts with their advisers.

In addition to increasing financial resources and curriculum flexibility, colleges can help to prevent severe stress in students by teaching them about a wide range of skills, including study skills, test-taking strategies, effective time management, and specific stress-management methods, such as relaxation or exercise. Students can also be encouraged to make effective use of whatever social support is available to them, and they can be taught the importance of sharing difficult feelings and concerns with others in appropriate ways. Interpersonal skills training, as well as information about the health benefits of social relationships, could enable students to use support systems effectively as a buffer against stress. It may also be useful to increase the involvement of students with one another—in class, for example, through more small-group interaction, or outside class through the development of interactive campus activities. These sorts of steps could facilitate the development of campus friendships and enrich the learning experience. Finally, information on good health habits, including sleep, nutrition, and exercise, may increase the well-being of students, particularly if such information is geared toward the immediate benefits of stress management and enhanced well-being, as opposed to the long-term benefits.

As for interventions with students who are already experiencing stress, the availability of brief individualized psychotherapy for students in crisis, as well as of extended psychotherapy for those who need it, is essential, since crises can bring out deeper issues for students, as well as opportunities for personal growth that are often effectively developed in therapy. Housing complexes often have students serve as resident assistants, with responsibility for student welfare. These individuals can fill an important immediate role by intercepting students who are experiencing unusual amounts of stress. They should be well informed about sources of stress on campus and about the various means of assistance. It may also be useful to form voluntary groups for students, where they can discuss their stress-related concerns. Much like self-help groups, these groups could be formed at the start of each quarter or semester, with between eight and twelve participants who would attend weekly sessions with a facilitator. The groups could be especially effective in helping with the management of chronic stress because they would legitimize discussions of the stressors that ebb and flow over time.

A final suggestion for addressing stress among students is to develop sanctioned programs, whereby students could take a quarter or a year off if the circumstances of their lives were not conducive to learning. Many students could benefit from this time away, especially if they were helped to obtain career-related work experience and to work out the details of their time away.

Conclusion

We have argued for the evidence that many college students today are experiencing high levels of stress. This picture does not match the traditional image of college as an easy time. Compared to college students of two decades ago, students today appear to be experiencing more and different kinds of stress. There are also signs that the stress experienced by college students today is similar in amount and type to that found in the general population. Students confront substance abuse, illness, death, loneliness, and depression. Some types of stress are unusually prevalent on college campuses, such as stressors related to sexual assault, eating disorders, and suicide. Perhaps most important is the possibility that the quality of the learning experience for many students is impaired by life stress. In this chapter, we have tried to emphasize the need for further systematic investigation of these issues and to suggest ways to go about it. Programs aimed at reducing stress should improve the quality of student life and simultaneously enhance the learning opportunities afforded by attending college.

References

Abbey, A., Abramis, D. J., and Caplan, R. D. "Effects of Different Sources of Social Support and Social Conflict on Emotional Well-Being." *Basic and Applied Social Psychology*, 1985, *6*, 119–129.

Antonovsky, A. *Health, Stress, and Coping: New Perspectives on Mental and Physical Well-Being.* San Francisco: Jossey-Bass, 1979.

Astin, A. W., Green, K. C., Korn, W. S., Schalit, M., and Berz, E. R. *The American Freshman: National Norms for Fall 1988.* Los Angeles: Higher Education Research Institute, University of California, 1988.

Beard, S. S., Elmore, R. T., and Lange, S. "Assessment of Student Needs: Areas of Stress in the Campus Environment." *Journal of College Student Personnel*, 1982, *23*, 348–350.

Bernard, M. L., and Bernard, J. L. "Suicide on Campus: Response to the Problem." In E. S. Zinner (ed.), *Coping with Death on Campus.* New Directions for Student Services, no. 31. San Francisco: Jossey-Bass, 1985.

Brennan, A. F., Walfish, S., and AuBuchon, P. "Alcohol Use and Abuse in College Students. II. Social/Environmental Correlates, Methodological Issues, and Implications for Intervention." *International Journal of the Addictions*, 1986, *21*, 475–493.

Cebelin, M. S., and Hirsch, C. S. "Human Stress Cardio-Myopathy—Myocardial Lesions in Victims of Homicidal Assaults Without Internal Injuries." *Human Pathology*, 1980, *11*, 123–132.

Christenfeld, R., and Black, H. K. "Mental Health and the Quiet Campus." *Social Psychiatry*, 1977, *12*, 117–125.

Cohen, S., and Hoberman, H. H. "Positive Events and Social Supports as Buffers of Life Change Stress." *Journal of Applied Social Psychology*, 1983, *13*, 99–125.

Cohen, S., Karmarck, T., and Mermelstein, R. "A Global Measure of Perceived Stress." *Journal of Health and Social Behavior*, 1983, *24*, 385–396.

Compas, B. E., Wagner, B. M., Slavin, L. A., and Vannatta, K. "A Prospective Study of Life Events, Social Support, and Psychological Symptomatology During the Transition from High School to College." *American Journal of Community Psychology*, 1986, *14*, 241–257.

Comstock, L. K., and Slome, C. "A Health Survey of Students: Prevalence of Perceived Problems." *Journal of the American College Health Association*, 1973, *22*, 150–155.

Cutrona, C. E. "Transition to College: Loneliness and the Process of Social Adjustment." In L. A. Peplau and D. Perlman (eds.), *Loneliness: A Sourcebook of Current Theory, Research, and Therapy*. New York: Wiley, 1982.

DeLongis, A., Coyne, J. C., Dakof, G., Folkman, S., and Lazarus, R. S. "Relationship of Daily Hassles, Uplifts, and Major Life Events to Health Status." *Health Psychology*, 1982, *1*, 119–136.

Edmunds, G. J. "Needs Assessment Strategy for Black Students: An Examination of Stressors and Program Implications." *Journal of Non-White Concerns in Personnel and Guidance*, 1984, *12*, 48–56.

Fleming, J. "Stress and Satisfaction in College Years of Black Students." *Journal of Negro Education*, 1981, *50*, 307–318.

Fowler, F. J., Jr. *Survey Research Methods*. Vol. 1. Applied Social Research Methods Series. Newbury Park, Calif.: Sage, 1984.

Frey, J. H. *Survey Research by Telephone*. Vol. 150. Sage Library of Social Research. Newbury Park, Calif.: Sage, 1983.

Gatchel, R. J., Baum, A., and Krantz, D. S. *An Introduction to Health Psychology*. New York: Random House, 1989.

Grant, I., Sweetwood, H., Yager, J., and Gerst, M. S. "Patterns in the Relationship of Life Events and Psychiatric Symptoms Over Time." *Journal of Psychosomatic Research*, 1978, *22*, 183–191.

Gunnings, B. B. "Stress and the Minority Student on a Predominantly White Campus." *Journal of Non-White Concerns in Personnel and Guidance*, 1982, *11*, 11–16.

Hobfoll, S. E. "Conservation of Resources: A New Attempt at Conceptualizing Stress." *American Psychologist*, 1989, *44* (3), 515–524.

Ionescu, R., and Popescu, C. "Stressful Life Events Associated with Depressive Syndromes Onset in Student Population." *Neurologie et Psychiatrie*, 1986, *24*, 105–112.

Jacobson, G. F. "Programs and Techniques of Crisis Intervention." In G. Caplan (ed.), *American Handbook of Psychiatry: Child and Adolescent Psychiatry, Sociocultural and Community Psychiatry*. (2nd ed.) New York: Basic Books, 1974.

Jacobson, G. F. "Crisis Oriented Therapy." *Psychiatric Clinics of North America,* 1979, *2,* 39–54.

Jemmott, J. B., III, and Locke, S. E. "Psychosocial Factors, Immunologic Mediation, and Human Susceptibility to Infectious Diseases: How Much Do We Know?" *Psychological Bulletin,* 1984, *95,* 78–108.

Kanner, A. D., Coyne, J. C., Schaeffer, C., and Lazarus, R. S. "Comparison of Two Modes of Stress Measurement: Daily Hassles and Uplifts Versus Major Life Events." *Journal of Behavioral Medicine,* 1981, *4,* 1–39.

Kessler, R. C., Price, R. H., and Wortman, C. B. "Social Factors in Psychopathology: Stress, Social Support, and Coping Processes." *Annual Review of Psychology,* 1985, *36,* 531–572.

Koplik, E. K., and DeVito, A. J. "Problems of Freshmen: Comparison of Classes of 1976 and 1986." *Journal of College Student Personnel,* 1986, *27,* 124–131.

LaGrand, L. E. "College Student Loss and Response." In E. S. Zinner (ed.), *Coping with Death on Campus.* New Directions for Student Services, no. 31. San Francisco: Jossey-Boss, 1985.

Lazarus, R. S. *Psychological Stress and the Coping Process.* New York: McGraw-Hill, 1966.

Lazarus, R. S., and Folkman, S. *Stress, Appraisal, and Coping.* New York: Springer, 1984.

Lazarus, R. S., and Launier, R. "Stress-Related Transactions Between Person and Environment." In L. A. Rervin and M. Lewis (eds.), *Perspectives in Interactional Psychology.* New York: Plenum, 1978.

Lecompte, D. "Emotional Distress in a First-Year University Population." *Acta Psychiatrica Belgica,* 1986, *86,* 64–70.

Mechanic, D., and Greenley, J. R. "The Prevalence of Psychological Distress and Help-Seeking in a College Student Population." *Social Psychiatry,* 1976, *11,* 1–14.

Moos, R. H., and Van Dort, B. "Physical and Emotional Symptoms and Campus Health Center Utilization." *Social Psychiatry,* 1977, *12,* 107–115.

Myers, H. F., Bastien, R. T., and Miles, R. E. "Life Stress, Health, and Blood Pressure in Black College Students." *Journal of Black Psychology,* 1983, *9,* 1–25.

"The Perils of Burnout." *Newsweek on Campus,* October 1987, pp. 5–10.

Pinch, W. J., Heck, M., and Vinal, D. "Health Needs and Concerns of Male Adolescents." *Adolescence,* 1986, *21,* 961–969.

Pliner, J. E., and Brown, D. "Projections of Reactions to Stress and Preference for Helpers Among Students from Four Ethnic Groups." *Journal of College Student Personnel,* 1985, *26,* 147–151.

Pyle, R. L., Halvorson, A., Neuman, P. A., and Mitchell, H. E. "The Increasing Prevalence of Bulimia in Freshman College Students." *International Journal of Eating Disorders,* 1986, *5,* 631–648.

Radloff, L. S. "The CES-D Scale: A Self Report Depression Scale for Research in General Populations." *Applied Psychological Measurement,* 1977, *1,* 385–401.

Reifler, C. B. "Epidemiologic Aspects of College Mental Health." *Journal of the American College Health Association,* 1971, *19,* 159–163.

Reifman, A., and Dunkel-Schetter, C. "Stress, Structural Social Support, and Well-Being in University Students." *American Journal of College Health,* in press.

Rook, K. "The Negative Side of Social Interaction: Impact on Psychological Well-Being." *Journal of Personality and Social Psychology,* 1984, *46,* 1097–1108.

Sherer, M. "Depression and Suicidal Ideation in College Students." *Psychological Reports,* 1985, *57,* 1061–1062.

Shure, G. H., and Meeker, R. J. "A Minicomputer System for Multiperson Computer-Assisted Telephone Interviewing." *Behavior Research Methods and Instrumentation,* 1978, *10,* 196–202.

Stokes, J. "Drug Use Among Undergraduate Psychology Students at an Urban University." *Drug Forum,* 1974, *3,* 335–359.

"The Stress Syndrome: Burnout to Suicide." *Newsweek on Campus,* December 1983, pp. 24–26.

Surtees, P. G., and Ingham, J. G. "Life Stress and Depressive Outcome: Application of a Dissipation Model to Life Events." *Social Psychiatry,* 1980, *15,* 21–31.

Thompson, J. R., Bentz, W. K., and Liptzin, M. B. "The Prevalence of Psychiatric Disorder in an Undergraduate Population." *Journal of the American College Health Association,* 1973, *21,* 415–422.

Tracey, T. J., Sherry, P., and Keitel, M. "Distress and Help-Seeking as a Function of Person-Environment Fit and Self-Efficacy: A Causal Model." *American Journal of Community Psychology,* 1986, *14,* 657–676.

Wechsler, H., Rohman, M. A., and Solomon, L. "Emotional Problems and Concerns of New England College Students." *American Journal of Orthopsychiatry,* 1981, *51,* 719–723.

Wortman, C., and Dunkel-Schetter, C. "Conceptual and Methodological Issues in the Study of Social Support." In A. Baum and J. E. Singer (eds.), *Handbook of Psychology and Health.* Hillsdale, N.J.: Erlbaum, 1987.

Zitzow, D. "The College Adjustment Rating Scale." *Journal of College Student Personnel,* 1984, *25,* 160–164.

Christine Dunkel-Schetter is an associate professor of psychology at the University of California, Los Angeles. She has conducted research on stress, social support, and coping among medical students, pregnant women, and cancer patients, as well as among undergraduates, for the past seven years.

Marci Lobel recently earned a Ph.D. degree in social and health psychology from the University of California, Los Angeles. Her doctoral research was on biopsychosocial factors, including stress, that influence pregnancy and childbirth.

We often do not see a student with drug and alcohol problems
until he or she meets a crisis or "hits bottom."

The Problem of Substance Abuse

Vivian B. Brown

Drug and alcohol use is one of the major problems in the country and on the college campus. Studies show that college students drink more than other groups in the population, may drink more at one time, and tend to use illegal drugs (O'Malley, Bachman, and Johnston, 1988; Johnston, O'Malley, and Bachman, 1987). Results of the most recent annual College Alcohol Survey showed that 35 percent of student-affairs administrators thought campus problems involving alcohol had increased in the past several years, and 41 percent saw no change (Magner, 1988). When a similar survey was conducted in 1985, 30 percent said alcohol-related problems had increased.

The issue of crisis is an important concept for substance use, misuse, and abuse because we often do not see a student in the counseling center until he or she meets a crisis or "hits bottom." Until something has changed in the student's life, he or she will not seek counseling, particularly regarding drugs and alcohol. It is extremely important that all counseling center staff be knowledgeable about patterns of use, drugs of abuse, how to take a comprehensive drug history (how to ask the right questions), and how to work with denial.

Two major crisis situations bring a substance abuser into counseling: (1) when the drugs or alcohol get the individual in trouble with the law, school, a job, or significant others (drugs as precipitant), and (2) when some event causes the student to increase drinking or drugging, and this leads to more serious problems, such as an overdose or the need for emergency medical attention (drugs as coping). In either case, we see the student when something has gone wrong and he or she cannot keep up the denial that there is no problem. When the drinking or drugging has gotten out of control, the student may seek help, even though the presenting problem may be something entirely different from drugs.

In this chapter, we look at substance use and abuse as both a coping mechanism for dealing with crises (self-medicating) and as a precipitant to crises.

Assessment

As a natural part of the intake process for the counseling center, students should be asked about their use of substances. This involves use of alcohol, illegal drugs, prescribed medications, and over-the-counter drugs. Given the extent of alcohol and drug use in students, and given the denial that often characterizes the person with drug and alcohol problems, it is best to assume that the student uses some substance until the truth is proved to be otherwise. In this way, the counselor will be able to assess what, if any, role drugs or alcohol play in the presenting problem.

It is also important to understand the substance use-misuse-abuse continuum. Many students may use substances. They may have a beer at a party, smoke a joint before a concert, or take an amphetamine to study for an important exam. This use may not cause a problem for the student, even though he or she is using an illegal substance in only one instance. Nevertheless, it is not free of risk. Use of an illegal substance can lead to arrest, and use of other substances can cause physiological changes that may be deleterious. As the student turns toward increased *use* of drugs or alcohol, and as we see some beginning signs of problematic behaviors (such as driving under the influence or taking twice the prescribed dose of a tranquilizer), we see the student move toward *misuse*. *Abuse* is defined as a pattern of pathological use (misuse), for at least a month, that causes impairment in social or occupational functioning.

These distinctions appear quite straightforward. However, we now know that there are some students who are more vulnerable than others to the effects of chemicals. One group of vulnerable students includes those who are adult children of alcoholics (ACAs) or who come from households with an addicted family member. Another more vulnerable group of students includes those with severe emotional disorders. Recent research indicates that for the young adult with diagnoses of schizophrenia and manic-depressive disorder (Pepper and Ryglewicz, 1982), even the smallest amount of a drug may be too much. This student may end up in a psychiatric hospital after one drink or one dose of cocaine. The assessment of a drug and/or alcohol problem does not depend solely on a diagnosis of abuse.

With regard to the assessment process, if the student is not a chronic user or abuser, crisis intervention can have considerable impact on use and misuse. If the student is an abuser, crisis services also can have considerable impact, but not in the same way. The crisis gives us the opportunity to assist the student in stopping denial—it is intervention at its best. Recovery is a lifelong process; the turn toward abstinence is a crisis period.

Intervention

As already stated, a student is most likely to come to the counseling center when she or he is in trouble with substances, either directly or indirectly. The detective work in the first session involves finding out whether there has been some hazardous event that led the student to increase drug or alcohol use, or whether the student's substance use has itself become a hazardous circumstance.

For example, Donna came to the counseling center after being referred by the emergency room at the university hospital. She was taken to the hospital by her roommate, who was afraid that Donna was "going crazy"; Donna had begun to talk about killing herself or someone else after taking "only one hit off a joint." Neither the roommate nor Donna could understand what had happened.

As another example, John came to the center in an extremely agitated state. He had not been sleeping well for a few nights and was afraid he might be "losing it." When asked about his drug and alcohol history, he said that he had used many drugs, including marijuana, LSD, Ecstasy, and amphetamines. He had stopped all drugs a "few nights ago" because he had passed out, or had "a blackout," and become quite frightened. When the counselor focused on whether there had been any change in his drug taking, he stated that he had increased his use when his girlfriend left him, the week before. At that time, he "didn't want to think or feel and got loaded."

Another student, Judy, came to the center after a weekend-long alcohol binge. She did not remember what had happened, only that her friends and her roommate questioned where she had stayed. She felt frightened because this reminded her of her father's blackouts when he was drinking.

Finally, Ronny, who was a member of an intercollegiate weightlifting team, was referred by his coach for steroid use. He was angry and agitated as he told the counselor that he had been suspended from the team. He knew that steroids were prohibited, but he said, "Everyone uses them, and I have been a champion because of them."

These four case examples reflect the types of crises that bring students to our attention. For every student coming to the counseling center, there are potentially many others who are not asking for help. Crisis intervention with these problems focuses on (1) breaking through the denial regarding drug or alcohol use, (2) assessing the extent to which substances are a means of coping with another crisis (self-medicating) or the sole crisis (disease), (3) assisting the student in understanding what effects drugs or alcohol have on his or her behavior, and (4) supporting the turn toward abstinence. It is important to get the student to abstain for the period of the crisis intervention. This can be put into an "experimental" framework: "Would you be willing to experiment for the six-week period and not use any drugs or alcohol?" In this way, the student experiences a period of being "clean and sober" and works on resolving the crisis in a more adaptive way. This period also allows the counselor to point out the significant changes that occur when the student is not using drugs.

No matter how clear-cut the existence of long-term drug abuse may be, we must keep in mind that the student has lived with this for periods of time without seeking help. People seek help when life changes have sufficiently disturbed them. With drug users, there is often a chain reaction because the way that one crisis is resolved (use of drugs) may create new problems. For example, once heavy drinking is under way, the student's life becomes more complicated. Heavy drinking episodes trigger other consequences, such as family problems, interpersonal conflicts, and school problems. These problems in turn trigger drinking bouts.

As part of the detective work in the first session of crisis intervention, it is helpful to put together a timeline, outlining the precipitating event and some of the relevant antecedent events. I begin with the student's first contact with the counseling center (extreme left of the timeline) and then, with the student-client, I move back and forth, identifying events and plotting them on the timeline. Events are recorded as far back in time as is necessary to understand the picture of the current crisis. In this way, the student understands what we are looking for, in terms of precipitating events, and becomes an active participant in identifying relevant events. Students and other clients often find it very helpful to see their recent life mapped out before them; the timeline makes the crisis work more understandable and accurate. I have seen clients suddenly remember an event, which was first omitted in the timeline, when they were able to see the chronology before their eyes.

If we use the case example of John, we would begin to plot the timeline as follows:

First contact	Not sleeping	Blackout	Girlfriend left him

The timeline also gives us a good picture of some of the important issues to explore with John, such as when he began his drug use, what other losses of relationships he has experienced, how he coped with those events, and whether he had any other blackouts. It would be important to reinforce John's abstention from drug use during his work in counseling and to help him ventilate the feelings he does not want to feel. It appears that John needs assistance with grieving—both the loss of his girlfriend and the loss of his drug use. The latter loss is important and often overlooked in counseling. If this loss is not explored, it is likely that John will relapse.

My crisis formulation to John would be as follows: "John, for many situations in your life, you have coped by using drugs. When your girlfriend left, you increased your drug taking until it became a problem for you—you blacked out. So you got scared and stopped the drugs, but that also caused you to feel upset. So you're in a no-win situation." I would then listen carefully to his response. He would tell me if this formulation made any sense to him and why or why not.

In the case of Donna, I would focus on a number of issues. What did the staff at the emergency room tell Donna about the crisis situation? What did it mean to Donna that her roommate thought she was "going crazy"? Had the same situation ever happened before—that she had smoked some marijuana and lost control? What did that mean to Donna? Had any other event happened right before this situation? Had there been any other hospitalizations? All of these issues may lead to important paths related to the crisis situation. My hypothesis would be that Donna took the marijuana to be like her roommate and peers and that, because of her vulnerability (emotional disorder), she could not tolerate the drug and lost control. Both she and her roommate then became frightened. The referral by the emergency room staff might have confirmed both of their fears that Donna was "crazy." My intervention would focus on checking out this hypothesis. If it appeared correct, then I would assist Donna in understanding that she cannot tolerate drugs and/or alcohol the way her friends do, that she may need to find other ways to be part of the group, and that she may need to participate in activities with other students who also do not tolerate drugs too well.

In the case of Judy, I would focus on the meaning of her blackout and failure to remember what happened over the weekend. My hypothesis would be that she is now frightened about possibly being like her father, who is an alcoholic. If this hypothesis were correct, we would have a break in the denial regarding her drinking. Is this the first time that she has blacked out? What does she fear happened? What were the circumstances that led to the binge? My intervention would focus on assisting Judy in understanding that her drinking is now problematic and that she may need to address her drinking behavior.

In the case of Ronny, I would help him deal with his loss and his anger that other people may be using steroids and going undetected. The possibility of Ronny's reinstatement on the team could be used to assist him in abstaining from steroid use. Without this motivation, it would become a much more difficult task. This difficulty is particularly acute in cases where the student is quite successful and drug use is associated with his or her success (an association often implied in athletics). The goal of the intervention with Ronny would be to help him understand the negative consequences of steroid use and the reasons for the prohibitions.

Many staff members of counseling centers feel uncomfortable with their lack of training in substance abuse issues, as well as with the traditional message that alcoholics and addicts do not do well in psychotherapy. Training in substance abuse issues is quite important for all staff, and it should include a component dealing with attitudes toward substance abusers. Counselors often feel anxious that they will not get the "right" crisis formulation. In crisis work, the student-client will play an active role in formulating the crisis. What is important is that the counselor stay within a crisis framework. In addition, staff may believe that one cannot help drug abusers or alcoholics in six sessions. However, students who abuse drugs and/or alcohol will do well in crisis intervention if counselors see themselves as part of a much larger intervention system. While the focus in individual crisis intervention is on assisting in the breaking through of denial and distortion and on supporting the turn toward abstinence, the simultaneous use of other support systems is quite critical. This partnership of support is important, both for intervention and for relapse prevention.

Crisis Groups. An effective modality for drug problems is the crisis group. In this intervention, all group participants share a common problem: drug and/or alcohol abuse (Brown, 1971). It is a powerful modality because the intervener works with a number of members who are at the point of breaking through their denial and taking active steps to work on changing their behavior. Group members help one another see how drugs have affected their behavior, support one another in the turn toward abstinence, help to provide alternative coping strategies, and help in behavioral rehearsal of new skills. In the crisis group, the intervener or counselor is truly an active facilitator. It is important that every member of the group have a chance to participate during every session, since the maximum time is six weeks.

The crisis group also substitutes people for drugs and the drug subculture. Students who use drugs are often enmeshed in an entire drug-using system. If they give up drugs and alcohol, they also lose or must give up many of their friends. At that point, they feel alone, and the pull back to drugs is quite strong. The crisis group provides experience with another set of friends—neither completely "straight" nor completely "stoned" (Brown, 1971).

Twelve-Step Approach. It is important, as part of the intervention, to encourage students to attend Alcoholics Anonymous (AA) and similar meetings, on or off campus. In some instances, students may prefer to attend meetings away from the campus, where they will not be recognized. In AA the individual will hear a clear behavioral message: "Don't take the first drink, stay away from slippery places, and go to ninety meetings in ninety days." They will also hear a cognitive message: "I am an alcoholic" (Brown, 1985). In addition to reinforcing cognitive-behavioral congruity, AA provides the foundation for lifelong recovery. Crisis intervention helps the student to participate in this new coping strategy.

Prevention Strategies

Drug and alcohol education and prevention programs have been implemented on many campuses. Some of the better-known programs are BACCHUS (Boost Alcohol Consciousness Concerning the Health of University Students), a national not-for-profit organization with local chapters (Gonzalez, 1986); the Demonstration Alcohol Education Project (DAEP) at the University of Massachusetts (Kraft, 1984); and the Total Alcohol Awareness Program (TAAP) at Pennsylvania State University (Upcraft and Eck, 1986). These programs provide an educational format for the entire campus. Their aim is to prevent drug and alcohol problems.

In addition to educational programs, most colleges and universities have adopted stricter alcohol policies for the campus, including the forbidding of hazing, clear guidelines for alcohol marketing on campus, and guidelines for social activities. These efforts have been greatly expanded in the past few years, and we are beginning to learn what the more effective strategies are for preventing or reducing drug and alcohol problems on campus. The following sections describe strategies for prevention programming.

Comprehensive Focus. It is interesting to note that many colleges and universities focus on alcohol. It may be reasoned that alcohol is used most frequently and is a greater problem, and so there should be a focus on alcohol. Nevertheless, it is equally important to realize that (1) polydrug use, misuse, and abuse are now quite common throughout the country, (2) marijuana has been the second drug of choice, (3) cocaine use is on the rise, (4) misuse of prescription drugs is common practice, (5) many students believe that Ecstasy and other "designer drugs" are quite safe (safer than alcohol), and (6) the use of steroids among athletes is quite common. The entire range of drugs needs to be the focal point of drug awareness programs on campus. While there are strong similarities across substances with regard to responsible use and abstinence, there are some major differences, and these should not be underplayed. Differences include life-style issues (legal drugs versus illegal drugs), mode of substance use (needle use versus drinking), and health risks (known risks of alcohol versus unknown risks of Ecstasy). If these issues are not discussed honestly with the students who are using these substances, the students will not trust the message or the messenger.

Focus on High-Risk Students. It is also important to focus educational efforts on high-risk students (ACAs, students who are depressed, students with more severe emotional disorders) and on high-risk situations (drinking and driving, date-rape situations in which alcohol plays an important part, experiments with new substances). Specialized groups can be implemented in the counseling center and in the residence halls. These groups can have an educational workshop format and a structured curriculum that allows for expression of students' experiences and feelings. Faculty members can include drug and alcohol education in the curriculum whenever it is appropriate. For example, in health classes, instructors can discuss the physiological effects of drug and alcohol, the effects when an individual is depressed, and the effects when a student is driving or taking an examination. In psychology classes, instructors can bring up the issue of denial in drug and alcohol abuse, the treatment strategies for substance abuse, and prevention strategies.

Campuswide prevention programming can include a drug awareness week, large media events, drug-free activities, and drug-free rush in fraternities and sororities. Campus newspapers can carry ongoing articles on drug and alcohol issues, including recent research findings.

Focus on What Is Known and Not Known. I have found it very helpful to be able to relate my own experiences in drug prevention and treatment over twenty-five years, beginning with my work in the 1960s and with LSD. I have never found students unwilling to discuss drug and alcohol issues when they believe that we are (1) not trying to tell them to "just say no," (2) knowledgeable about the topic and willing to say what is known and what is not known at this time (with the recognition that this is always changing, cocaine and crack being excellent examples), and (3) understand that they wish to experiment with drugs during their college years but do not wish to "mess up their heads."

Peer Programming. Peer counseling and education is another important strategy in drug and alcohol education and prevention. Many campuses are using a peer counselor/health advocate model to get messages out across the entire college community. Peers can go into sorority and fraternity houses, residence halls, and student organizations to deliver prevention messages. From recent experience with AIDS prevention, for example, we now know that—in addition to the health-belief model emphasizing the consequences of drug and alcohol abuse, the probability that these consequences will occur, and the effectiveness of a recommended coping response—the most effective strategy is to have coping messages delivered by peers from the targeted individuals' support system. (Thus, it has been shown that in delivering AIDS-prevention messages about safer sex and condom use, this effort was most effective if the targeted individuals knew that their peers were utilizing these coping responses.)

Drugs and Alcohol in the Context of Stress. I have found it extremely helpful to discuss substance use from a stress-management perspective. Beginning with freshman orientation, students can participate in stress-management workshops, using role playing of common stressful events (first bad grade, first fraternity party). With such role playing, it is easy for the facilitator to include the use of drugs and alcohol as means of coping with anxiety or stress. These discussions can be continued throughout the year for all students, in their residence halls, their organizations, and so on.

Community Focus. While it is clear that drugs and alcohol are a problem for students across the country, it is important not to deny that they are also a problem for staff and faculty on the campus. Drug awareness programs need to be campuswide and, ideally, to include not only all members of the campus community but also their family members. The new 1989 regulations on the drug-free workplace will affect many colleges and universities, and there will be increased emphasis on programming for drug awareness and employee assistance.

Conclusion

The issue of crisis is an important concept for drug and alcohol intervention and prevention. We often do not see a student in the counseling center until he or she meets a crisis. Substance use and abuse can be seen both as coping strategies for dealing with crises and as precipitants of crises.

It is important for counselors to understand the substance use-misuse-abuse continuum. Crisis intervention focuses on breaking through denial, helping the student understand the consequences for his or her functioning, and supporting the turn toward abstinence. Drug and alcohol prevention programs can also be based on the crisis model.

References

Brown, S. *Treating the Alcoholic: A Developmental Model of Recovery.* New York: Wiley, 1985.

Brown, V. B. "The Drug Crisis Group: Schizoid Personalities in Search of a Treatment." *Psychotherapy: Theory, Research and Practice,* 1971, *8* (3), 213–215.

Gonzalez, G. M. "Proactive Efforts and Selected Alcohol Education Programs." In T. G. Goodale (ed.), *Alcohol and the College Student.* New Directions for Student Services, no. 35. San Francisco: Jossey-Bass, 1986.

Johnston, L. D., O'Malley, P. M., and Bachman, J. G. *National Trends in Drug Use and Related Factors Among High School Students and Young Adults, 1975–1986.* Rockville, Md.: National Institute of Drug Abuse, 1987.

Kraft, D. P. "A Comprehensive Prevention Program for College Students." In P. M. Miller and T. D. Nirenberg (eds.), *Prevention of Alcohol Abuse.* New York: Plenum, 1984.

Magner, D. K. "Alcohol-Related Problems Have Not Decreased on Most College Campuses, Survey Indicates." *Chronicle of Higher Education,* November 9, 1988, pp. A35–A37.

O'Malley, P. M., Bachman, J. G., and Johnston, L. "Period, Age, and Cohort Effects on Substance Abuse Among Young Americans: A Decade of Change, 1976–86." *American Journal of Public Health,* 1988, 7 (10), 1315–1321.

Pepper, B., and Ryglewicz, H. (eds.). *The Young Adult Chronic Patient.* New Directions for Mental Health Services, no. 14. San Francisco: Jossey-Bass, 1982.

Upcraft, M. L., and Eck, W. "TAAP: A Model Alcohol Education Program that Works." In T. G. Goodale (ed.), *Alcohol and the College Student.* New Directions for Student Services, no. 35. San Francisco: Jossey-Bass, 1986.

Vivian B. Brown is chief executive officer of PROTOTYPES, a center for innovation in health, mental health, and social services. She is also a consultant for student psychological services at the University of California, Los Angeles, and for substance abuse prevention at the California Institute of Technology.

Crisis intervention is an approach that can enable the client and the counselor to intervene actively during times of suicidal crisis.

Crisis Intervention and Prevention with Suicide

Harold L. Pruett

> Julie is a nineteen-year-old sophomore. On Wednesday, she will climb to the top of a university parking structure and jump to her death. The tragedy will not end there. Her friends, roommates, professors, and fellow students will experience intense grief and question why a young person with such promise would kill herself.

Suicide has become the second most common cause of death among adolescents and young adults, ages fifteen to twenty-four. While many university and college students are older, a sizable group is within this age range, and most counseling and mental health programs on campus have found themselves increasingly concerned about suicidal students and about ways to prevent suicide, regardless of age.

While the reported incidence of completed suicides and suicide attempts varies, Schwartz and Reifler (1988, p. 58), in a comprehensive review of reported data on student suicide, conclude that, per year, "for a very large campus (e.g., 45,000 full-time students), one can anticipate about 5 suicides [and] 50 suicide attempts."

For many college students, suicide is a coping strategy that somehow seems better than the alternatives. We professionals and administrators, who can usually see many other alternatives, feel helpless when a student completes a suicide, and we look for someone to blame—usually ourselves. Although suicide on campus is still a relatively uncommon event, it is the one we fear the most.

New Directions for Student Services, no. 49, Spring 1990 © Jossey-Bass Inc., Publishers

The Crisis Model

Crisis intervention is an approach that can enable the counselor to intervene actively during a suicidal crisis. As a model of prevention, it not only can help us prevent suicide in the individuals we see in the counseling center but also can help us identify high-risk students on campus and intervene prior to some tragedy.

The concept of the crisis matrix (see Chapter One) can be very useful in further understanding suicide as a coping strategy in the college student. When the student enters the institution, he or she is already in a vulnerable state. The student is entering a new environment, may be leaving the parents' home or other familiar surroundings, and is faced with new challenges for which he or she may be ill prepared. The developmental transitions are complex and require new approaches. During this already vulnerable period, the student enters the institution and encounters many hazardous events that can precipitate a crisis. If the initial crisis is not resolved satisfactorily, the student's functioning will be compromised, and each new hazard (such as the first exam in which a lower grade than usual is received, or the first rejection from a member of the opposite sex) further taxes the student and leaves him or her functioning at a lower level than before. The student is more vulnerable to new hazards partly because of the developmental transitions he or she is experiencing. Coping strategies are finally exhausted, crises are unresolved, and suicide becomes a "final solution."

Prevention Programs

An adequate suicide-prevention program must contain several components. It must address the needs of the community, the administration, and the counseling center staff.

Administrative Component. The administration of the university or college needs to consider several issues, which are often ignored but require attention (personal communication, David Palmer, January 2, 1985). The institution must have an adequate emergency response system, first of all. This function usually consists of police or community safety units and paramedical units. A psychological component also should be included, so that assessment and follow-up can be performed. This component wil also assist the institution in dealing further with the event.

After the emergency response, there is the need to neutralize unpredictable behavior. The period immediately after the emergency response is most important for ensuring that the student is not going to harm himself or herself. The institution should have some mechanism to ensure that continued suicide prevention is taking place. This may be a hospital, although hospitalization is often neither available nor desirable. The mechanism will usually involve some form of outpatient response.

The third issue involves notification of someone designated by the student as a responsible party. For a young adult or late adolescent, this party may well be a parent but could also be a spouse or a friend. Notification of parents is often strongly opposed initially by the student ("My parents will be too upset"). Mental health professionals are also often resistant to notifying parents or others, for fear of breaching confidentiality. While we can certainly understand the concern, it is rare that contacting parents presents more of a problem than not contacting them. Solky, McKeever, Perlmutter, and Gift (1988) present some convincing material, indicating that notifying parents prior to hospitalization and including parents early in the treatment planning most often results in a productive intervention. They also indicate that "turmoil later in treatment" was always associated with the failure to work with the parents from the beginning. A parent most often can assist with the disposition following the emergency, and the mental health staff can often assist in resolving any issues between parent and child that require amelioration.

Confidentiality must be clearly addressed. At UCLA, we find it useful to confront the limits of confidentiality directly by having all student-clients sign a consent-to-treatment form after a discussion with a therapist that spells out the limits of confidentiality. One limit that we specify concerns when a student is considered to be a danger to himself or herself.

The institution should have some way of instituting constraints on disruptive behavior, so that the drain on resources is limited, particularly when there are a number of repetitions. This may take the form of behavioral contracting, required evaluations, exclusion from residence halls, and so on. It should not, in my opinion, include mandatory, psychiatrically grounded withdrawal from the institution.

A communication network is a vital part of any prevention or intervention program on campus and must be arranged so that those who need to be informed are not left out. Ordinarily, units and parties that need to be informed are the police, health providers, the counseling unit, the dean of students, residence hall staff, selected student-affairs officers, and, if possible, the public information officer and campus counsel. It is absolutely vital that units directly involved with a suicidal student communicate with one another, so that such a student does not fall through the cracks. A communication network provides for adequate concurrent consultation among the various institutional elements or services (often, such students will be in contact with three or four campus services at the same time). Such a network will also enable the various services to ascertain whether a current behavior is a repetition, what the previous response has been, and other important information.

Community Component. The needs of the community will vary but should certainly include information and education programs on early detection, training of caregivers and/or gatekeepers, and postvention and debriefing after completed suicides and suicide attempts.

Informational materials should be eye-catching and informative. Flyers, pamphlets, school newspapers, radio, films, and videotapes can be useful. Regardless of the particular medium chosen, simple written material, which can be distributed widely and possibly mailed out, should be included. At one point at UCLA, 20,000 single-page folded brochures were sent out to students, outlining basic suicide-prevention steps. Such a brochure should contain the following:

1. *The reasons for suicide.* Although there is no simple answer, we do know that suicidal students feel helpless and hopeless; their self-esteem is low. Suicidal crises do not occur in a vacuum and are related to events that almost always involve someone else: a breakup, change in a relationship, or loss of supports.

2. *Warning signs.* There are a number of warning signs to which people need to be alert. Examples include making threats to end one's life, giving away prized possessions, saying goodbye in various ways, exhibiting marked behavior changes, exhibiting marked lack of energy, and being increasingly isolated.

3. *What can you do?* Emphasis here is on listening to and expressing concern for someone who is exhibiting warning signs. Follow-up referrals should include phone numbers and availability. It is absolutely essential that availability of referral sources be checked.

Caregivers. Widespread training must occur with persons who have the most contact with students. Teaching assistants, tutors, advisers, and residence hall staff are all important gatekeepers. Student peers are always important, and training of students who work on hotlines, as advisers, and in residence halls is particularly important. Every year we see a number of students who are at risk and who have been referred to us by fellow students.

The content of such early-detection training usually consists of material similar to that included in information pamphlets. In general, it is important to dispel myths and provide clear instructions on what to do. These instructions specifically need to address what to say, as well as whom to contact when referring. Role playing is very important in training for listening skills.

Crisis Intervention

Prevention should be a priority, but when a student is identified as suicidal, either by himself or by someone else, it is necessary to have a crisis intervention component available to intervene as quickly as possible, so that the hazard can be identified and the healing process begun.

A key element of intervention is training. Providers of service must receive training in evaluation and crisis intervention. Evaluation must include a thorough understanding of the various risk factors that we know increase the possibility of suicide. In addition to a well-conceived plan, a statement of intent, and past attempts, other high-risk factors include suicide in the family, a history of psychiatric hospitalization, alienation from the family or another support net, alcohol and/or other substance use or abuse, feelings of hopelessness or helplessness, and difficulty in identifying the precipitant.

Determining whether a student who is suicidal can be managed on an outpatient basis is the first task of an intervener and depends on a number of factors: lethality of intent, support system available, willingness to make a nonsuicide agreement or contract, availability of the therapist, and degree of rapport between student and therapist. It is often at this stage that parents or significant others must be notified.

When a therapist is dealing with a highly lethal student and is considering hospitalization, outpatient treatment, or returning the student to the parental home, it is hardly the time to dwell on issues of individuation and separation. "While the individual developmental perspective is helpful for psychotherapy with students in an outpatient setting, emergency treatment and hospitalization require the addition of a family systems perspective" (Solky, McKeever, Perlmutter, and Gift, 1988).

Involving the family (there are, of course, exceptions) is often crucial: I believe that most suicidal behavior in late adolescence and young adulthood is related very directly to unresolved issues in the parent-child relationship. This view is not dissimilar to that expressed by family-systems therapists (Carter and McGoldrick, 1980; Arnstein, 1980). With older students, parents may not be as directly involved, but consideration of working with spouses and children is likewise important.

In assessing the suitability of outpatient treatment, it is helpful to use the technique described by Drye, Goulding, and Goulding (1973). Their technique essentially requires people to evaluate themselves and state that they will not attempt to kill themselves by accident or on purpose, no matter what happens. If a person can make such a statement with confidence, the therapist can usually assume that the person can be managed as an outpatient. Most suicidal individuals will make such a statement only if a time qualifier is used. The amount of time may vary from one or two hours to a week or more. Whether such a person can be managed then depends on the interval about which the therapist and client feel confident. I have often worked with people who were willing to make statements covering only two days, at the most.

It should be emphasized that any assessment of suicide, and any attempt to get a nonsuicide statement, must follow the building of adequate rapport. Often, this takes time. Establishing rapport with a suicidal student is exhausting and time-consuming, and any attempt to rush the process is doomed.

Occasionally, a therapist will not get a nonsuicide statement or other agreement from a client and will nevertheless proceed with the intervention. I believe that the first priority in working with a suicidal student is getting a clear nonsuicide agreement or statement. Without this, outpatient work cannot proceed. The student must realize how seriously we take him, and if a student cannot be trusted not to kill himself, then hospitalization obviously becomes the only reasonable alternative unless some type of twenty-four-hour monitoring is available (for example, by parents or a spouse). However, the burden this may place on nonprofessionals is great and may increase the risks.

Once the decision is made that the student can be seen outside the hospital, crisis intervention can proceed. In interventions with a student who is behaving suicidally, it becomes essential to identify the precipitating event, as well as the nature of the hazard represented by that event. In nearly all instances, this represents some form of loss. Losses may be related to nurturance or mastery. (We outlined the details of crisis intervention in Chapter One.)

Identification of the precipitating event is crucial if work is to proceed in a planned, focused direction. This step is also one of the most difficult, since the student is often unable (at least initially) to identify an event that has led to the suicidal ideation. When asked, "Why now?", students often say, "I just feel depressed" or "I've always felt this way."

The precipitating event, any antecedents, related events, and how past coping has broken down are important and essential pieces of information to determine if crisis intervention is to take place. When the therapist has sufficient information, the task is to help the student develop a cognitive grasp on how antecedent events have led to the current state of disequilibrium and feelings of hopelessness, helplessness, and despair, and to see how these have inspired the idea that suicide can lead to a solution by "ending it all." When did the idea come into being? What coping strategies have been available in the past that aren't available now? Has suicide been considered before? What were the circumstances? One obvious task is to help the student develop other, less self-destructive coping strategies.

While crises are time-limited, with four to six weeks being typical, the acute emergency is usually managed at a fast rate, within twenty-four to thirty-six hours. As discussed earlier, many students are in a vulnerable state, either because of developmental issues (for example, leaving home to go to college) or because of some trauma (for example, sexual assault) or preexisting pathology (for example, depression). In such a vulnerable state, students may experience multiple crises over an extended period. Students may exhibit acute suicidal behavior several times during this period of vulnerability, and crisis intervention must be readily available each time. Often such students have exhibited suicidal behavior in high school after a crisis, and that behavior has become one means of coping.

While intervention in the office or emergency room is crucial to resolving the suicidal crisis, the availability and use of social supports, including friends and family, will often determine the successful outcome.

Psychotropic medications can be a useful adjunct to crisis intervention, but care must obviously be taken that medication not be viewed as the magic that will make the pain go away. Avoidance of emotional pain is all too common a pattern.

Case Example

M. is a twenty-year-old woman who is a fourth-year junior. She works part-time and is also assisted financially by her mother. She came to the counseling center at the insistence of the friend who accompanied her. The friend announced to the therapist when they came in that M. was "depressed and talking about wanting to die."

During the initial evaluation, M. was quiet, with her eyes downcast; she never once made eye contact. When asked why she had come, she replied that her friend wanted her to come. She answered questions hesitatingly and volunteered nothing. She displayed very little affect but appeared clearly depressed.

"What happened that your friend decided that you needed to be seen?"

"We were just talking."

"Sounds like your friend is bothered by you talking about dying."

"I guess so."

"What has happened that you feel that way?"

"Not much."

"People don't feel that way out of the blue, and I would guess that something has happened, probably with another person, that has been very upsetting."

M. began to talk hesitatingly about her boyfriend, with whom she had recently broken up. She had been in the relationship for about nine months when he announced that he was going to start seeing other women. She reacted by withdrawing and finally stopped seeing him after a month. Initially, she denied any anger toward him.

In plotting a timeline with M., I saw that the breakup of the relationship had occurred two months before, and so it seemed unlikely that the breakup was the precipitating event, although it was certainly important. With substantial probing, M. was able to talk about a very recent encounter with her mother.

M. said she had always felt protective of her mother and had "always been there for her": "Mother has always relied on me." Following the breakup with her boyfriend, M. had been very distressed and had a minor traffic accident that resulted in some damage to another car.

Since M. was considered to be at fault, her mother's insurance company was being asked to cover the cost of repairs. In contrast to how she had expected her mother to act (warm, supportive, and understanding), her mother had scolded her, saying she was inconsiderate and always caused her trouble. M. felt devastated and betrayed. Feeling no anger toward either her mother or her boyfriend, she was aware only of intolerable anguish and a strong desire to die.

The suicide assessment was done, and M. had both a plan and the means to carry it out, but had not set any definite time. She seemed quite intent on suicide as a way both to relieve her burden and to get back at her boyfriend and her mother for hurting her so much.

The next step was to consider whether M. could safely be seen as an outpatient. She initially refused to make any nonsuicide statement, saying she could not and that it was a "stupid" thing to ask her to do. I said she sounded annoyed, and she replied, "I am."

"At me?"

"No."

"Then who?"

"Myself."

I challenged this assertion and asked her to tell me whom else she felt anger toward. With considerable support, she mentioned her mother and burst into tears.

She sobbed for some time and then asked why her mother had not been more supportive. After all these years, she had listened to her mother's complaints and had "always been there" for her. She talked some more about being disappointed and angry that her mother was "so insensitive." We then spent time identifying and talking about her guilt over having angry feelings toward her mother.

Having done some work on the feelings associated with the precipitant, I again brought up the issue of whether she was willing to be seen in the center or whether hospitalization needed to be considered. I asked if she could postpone any decision to commit suicide and could make a statement to that effect that would enable us to work on her feelings together. She was then willing to make such a statement, and we negotiated a series of visits to help work through her crisis over loss of nurturance.

Postvention

Tragically, suicide and serious suicide attempts do occur on campus. A suicide is not a normal death, and it leaves behind shattered lives. It is the ultimate form of abandonment. Survivors spend the rest of their lives wondering—and never knowing—whether they could have done something to prevent the tragedy. Suicide has a profound impact on the college and university community, and it is imperative that some sort of postvention take place. Postvention involves a number of steps, including identification of persons likely to be affected (friends, classmates, roommates, faculty, staff), selection of those who will facilitate debriefing and defusing, and selection of the time and place. Ideally, a campuswide protocol should be developed that spells out (among other items) a debriefing process. The membership of a protocol committee should include campus clergy, health care personnel, counseling center personnel, the dean of students, residence hall personnel, and campus police.

Arranging the meeting place and notifying those affected can be a logistical nightmare, but it is important. Those affected need to have an opportunity to participate, and they should be urged to do so. Defusing will usually occur as soon after the event as possible. If the suicide occurs in a residence hall, it is important to meet with the residence hall staff and then help them defuse the residents. The purpose of defusing should be to help people identify and discuss their feelings and reactions. It can be relatively unstructured. Campus clergy can also be an important resource for the defusing process.

Debriefing should occur one or two days after the event, although several debriefing sessions may be necessary over a period of one or two weeks. (See Chapter One for a description of the debriefing process.) The debriefing outline cannot be followed when the group is a large one (for example, an entire floor of a residence hall), and so the format will become more educational. The importance of assisting survivors who are affected by the suicide of a student cannot be overemphasized. We often forget that the impact is similar to ripples created when a stone is tossed into the water. Those ripples extend significantly beyond the immediate survivors. Survivors need help expressing feelings (often guilt and anger), understanding those feelings and their reactions, reviewing experiences with the deceased, and discussing strategies for dealing with their feelings. Again, campus clergy may be an important resource, as may campus health care personnel, provided that they have had some training in debriefing. In each instance, normalizing survivors' feelings and reactions is very important.

Case Example

J. was a twenty-three-year-old male graduate student who jumped from the building that housed his department. J. was a new student who had just completed his first quarter at UCLA. His academic work was somewhat questionable, and a number of problems were evident. He had not been seen for treatment. He jumped at noon, a busy time when a great deal of foot traffic was passing by the building. His tragic leap was witnessed by several people, mostly strangers.

Because he had jumped at midday and was well known within his department, several steps were immediately initiated. A team of staff from the counseling center was dispatched to the scene within minutes of his jump. At the same time, the departmental chair was contacted, and arrangements were set in motion to meet with several staff, who initially were the most affected. These people had either seen him jump or had seen him earlier in the day. A debriefing within the department for faculty and students was scheduled within two days.

Since J. lived in a residence hall, the director of residential life was contacted, and arrangements were made to debrief the entire residence hall. A counseling center staff person met with J.'s roommate as soon as the latter could be located. Three debriefings were held in the residence hall; the first was conducted on the evening of the day J. jumped.

In addition to scheduling the debriefings, we tracked J.'s activities, to see how far the ripples extended, and we identified two student groups that also needed debriefing. There followed an article in the school newspaper, and we inserted a brief statement after the article, requesting anyone who needed to talk to contact either the counseling center or the anonymous student "HELPline." Finally, a debriefing was held for all campus services that were involved in dealing with the suicide of J. These services included the police, residential life, student psychological services, and the office of the dean of students. The focus of the debriefing was on any institutional factors that might have needed to be addressed, such as communication problems and emergency response procedures. Modifications in the protocol were then made, as necessary.

References

Arnstein, R. L. "The Student, the Family, the University, and the Transition to Adulthood." *Adolescent Psychiatry*, 1980, *8*, 160–172.

Carter, E. A., and McGoldrick, M. (eds.). *The Family Life Cycle: A Framework for Family Therapy*. New York: Gardner Press, 1980.

Drye, R. C., Goulding, R. L., and Goulding, M. E. "No-Suicide Decisions: Patient Monitoring of Suicidal Risk." *American Journal of Psychiatry*, 1973, *130*, 171–174.

Schwartz, A. J., and Reifler, C. B. "College Student Suicide in the United States: Incidence Data and Prospects for Demonstrating the Efficacy of Preventative Programs." *Journal of the American College Health Association*, 1988, *37*, 53–59.

Solky, H. J., McKeever, J. E., Perlmutter, R. A., and Gift, T. E. "Involving Parents in the Management of Psychiatric Emergencies in College Students Far from Home." *Journal of the American College Health Association*, 1988, *36*, 335–339.

Harold L. Pruett, director of student psychological services at the University of California, Los Angeles, is also chair of the Organization of Counseling Center Directors in Higher Education in California and past president and fellow of the Los Angeles Society of Clinical Psychologists.

The primary goal of crisis work with victims of interpersonal violence is to restore coping and to assist their return to the previous level of functioning.

Interpersonal Violence and Crisis Intervention on the College Campus

Susan B. Sorenson, Vivian B. Brown

Recent events have increased the attention of universities and colleges to the problem of violence on their campuses. A 1987 lawsuit by the parents of a murdered coed challenged campuses to make public the available data concerning crime on campus (Hirschorn, 1987). In another testament to increased recognition of and sensitivity to this issue, Towson State University held its third national conference on campus violence in January 1989. The university's previous conferences had indicated that most violence on college campuses was primarily student-to-student violence, not imported by nonstudents (Sherrill and Siegel, 1989). Violence toward ethnic minority groups has increased on campuses, to such an extent that numerous articles have appeared in the popular press (for example, "Mass Protest," 1988).

The college campus operates within the context of the greater society. Therefore, the types of interpersonal crime and violence seen on campus parallel those seen off campus. Sexual assault, physical assault and battering, and crimes against groups (hate crimes) coexist with literature courses, football games, and fraternity rush. Statistics concerning violent crime (homicide, forcible rape, robbery, aggravated assault, and crimes against property) at public colleges and universities are gathered and published annually (for example, Federal Bureau of Investigation, 1988). Based on crimes known to police, these estimates do not describe unreported or undetected incidents; thus, they are likely to underestimate violence on campus.

This chapter outlines a general framework regarding violent victimization on college campuses. Most of the information we have on interpersonal campus violence is about rape; therefore, examples related to sexual victimization will be used in this chapter. Responses to other forms of violence are similar to those following sexual assault, yet they differ in important ways; space constraints limit the length and scope of these comments.

Magnitude of the Problem

Over thirty years ago, 26 percent of college men reported that they had forcefully attempted sexual intercourse with their dates, attempts that resulted in observable distress in the women (Kanin, 1957). More recent research with college men has shown that 15 percent acknowledge having engaged in sexual intercourse against their dates' will (Rapaport and Burkhart, 1984), while between 4.6 and 7.1 percent admit perpetrating sexual aggression that meets the legal definition of rape (Koss, 1985; Koss, Leonard, Beezley, and Oros, 1985; Koss and Oros, 1982; Koss, Gidycz, and Wisniewski, 1987; Muehlenhard and Linton, 1987). About one-third of male college students acknowledge some likelihood that they would rape a woman if they would not be caught (Malamuth, 1981).

On the basis of these reports from male college students, it is not surprising that reported rates of sexual assault are consistently high in samples of college women. A total of 20 to 25 percent of college women reported experiencing forceful attempts at sexual intercourse by their dates, in which the women ended up screaming, fighting, crying, or pleading (Kanin, 1957; Kanin and Parcell, 1977; Kirkpatrick and Kanin, 1957). A total of 13 to 14.7 percent of female college students reported experiencing sexual intercourse that took place without their consent and was accompanied by the use of force or the threat of harm (Koss, Gidycz, and Wisniewski, 1987; Muehlenhard and Linton, 1987).

Physical violence in dating relationships is also not rare (Aizenman and Kelley, 1988; Rouse, 1988). Spousal violence often begins in courtship (O'Leary and Arias, 1988), and so the college years can be thought of both as a high-risk time for establishing such patterns of violent interaction and as a good prevention point. Returning and nontraditional students may be in established relationships that include spousal violence or child abuse. Violence also occurs in other relationship contexts, such as between friends or strangers, and is not limited to male-to-female violence. For the purposes of this chapter, we will focus on forms of violence that are likely to be perpetuated in ongoing relationships, which are therefore likely to represent particularly important prevention points.

Underreporting of violent interactions is likely for at least four reasons. First, if the interaction is labeled unpleasant but not criminal (as is often the case in date rape), the victim is unlikely to consider herself a victim. Second, after such a victimization, the willingness to report or

seek assistance is reduced if the victim-s¹
done. Third, if the victim believes she ·
the assault may go unreported to auth
in situations involving student-victi⟩
backgrounds. Fourth, the political cc
enter in, including concerns abou
trayed by the media, understood
issues effectively reduces acknowle⌐⌐
on college campuses.

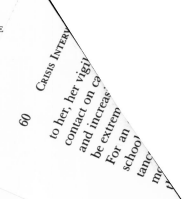

Intervention

Treatment and counseling of the victims of interpersonal violence ⌐
focus on the occurrence of and recovery from the event itself. The primai⟩
goal of the initial work with victims of violence is to restore coping and
assist return to the previous level of functioning. Thus, crisis intervention
is ideally suited to work with victims of violence.

The immediate problems include physical injury, threat to safety,
fear of pregnancy and sexually transmitted diseases (including AIDS),
and the risk of demeaning interactions with criminal justice and emergency room personnel. The victim also is at risk for delayed psychological reactions, including intrusive images of the event (Salasin, 1981;
Symonds, 1980), continuing fear, a sense of loss, depression, and the
potential for suicidal ideation (Sorenson and Golding, in press). Bard
and Sangrey (1986) hypothesize that victimization confronts both the
victim and those in her social milieu with a most unpleasant reality: that
one is never totally in control of one's life.

Common to all models describing victims' responses are feelings of
disorganization, fear, anger, denial, and shame. The reaction is best con-
ceived as a posttraumatic stress disorder that intensifies feelings of personal helplessness and vulnerability, which may lead to a revision of self-
concept and loss of self-esteem (Bard and Sangrey, 1986; for a review of
theoretical approaches to victims' reactions, see McCann, Sakheim, and
Abrahamson, 1988).

As outlined by Levy and Brown (1984), the specific objectives of
crisis intervention with victims of interpersonal violence are to assist the
victim in (1) retaining or regaining a sense of competence, (2) accepting
any uncontrollable consequences of the assault, (3) taking adaptive actions, including the maintenance of support systems, and (4) reestablish-
ing a sense of continuity and meaning in life. The goal of recovery is to
make the transition from victim to survivor.

With regard to fear, the sexual assault victim may report increased
anxiety and startle responses following the event. She may report fear of
being on campus alone or of being in a crowd. If the assailant is known

ance and fear may be stimulated by continued unexpected
mpus. For a young woman in the process of emancipation
ing independence, the sudden experience of vulnerability can
ely frightening and lead to renewed dependence on her parents.
older woman, the assault may amplify fears about returning to
and the costs of increased independence. The student needs assis-
in discussing fears and in developing a plan to both feel and be
re safe and secure. The counselor needs to assure the student-victim
at others have similar fears and that these feelings are a normal reaction
to an abnormal event.

As an extension of fear, the victim often feels that control of her life,
environment, safety, and ability to take care of herself has been seriously
threatened. This feeling of powerlessness results in new feelings of dependence; thus, an important task of the counselor is to encourage the
victim's active participation in treatment. This enhances the regaining
of feelings of power and mastery. The student-victim can be encouraged
to formulate a plan for making life tasks manageable and appropriately
paced.

Recovery from victimization is an extended process. This particular
"crisis matrix" (Levy and Brown, 1984; see Chapter One for further discussion) includes a number of periods during which crisis intervention
can assist in recovery. The matrix begins with the victimizing event and
the realization of personal damage, involves the reactions of others (including caregivers), and moves on to victimization-related events (such as
court appearances, if the event is reported to authorities and if the assailant is apprehended) and, finally, to the resumption of normal activity
(including dating and sexual activity for victims of sexual assault). Each
of these steps may precipitate another crisis period. It is important that
the counselor understand recovery as a series of potential crises.

Identifying events or times that could make healthy resolution problematic is an important part of termination. For example, if criminal
charges have been brought, then the pretrial, trial, and sentencing have
the potential of disrupting healthy resolution. The time of year also is
important. If the assault occurred during midterm week and the student's
performance on examinations was impaired, subsequent exams may pro-
voke anxiety. An anniversary appointment may be helpful, both to deal
with reawakened reactions and to mark the passing of a year of coping.

Sometimes additional treatment beyond resolution of the crisis is
both merited and desired. Such treatment should be conceptualized as
and presented to the client as distinct from the crisis that brought her
into treatment. The traumatic event may have served to awaken dormant
issues (such as a history of childhood sexual abuse), which now should
become the primary focus of continuing treatment.

Because sexual assault and battering most often are against women, the availability of sensitive women therapists is important for female students. Female therapists must be particularly aware of any desire to distance themselves from the student-victim and must avoid searching for something in the student that would make her culpable for the event. This introduces the issue of self-blame following victimization. Some research (Janoff-Bulman, 1979) indicates that behavioral (versus characterological) self-blame appears to help in the early restoration of previous functioning. Finding something one could have done differently serves to restore one's view of the world as predictable and controllable. This tendency is to be differentiated from characterological self-blame, in which the student-victim believes the attack was due to her personality characteristics or personal deficiencies. Recent research by Katz and Burt (1988) questions the need for self-blame as a path to regaining control. A majority of the victimized women in this study reported that counselors' statements that the women were not to blame were among the most helpful things they were told. Cognitive reframing of the event may help to impart a sense of competence and control (for example, "You did a good job of making choices that kept you from being hurt more severely") without focusing on self-blame.

Recovery from assault involving a known assailant differs in important ways from when an assailant is unknown (Katz and Burt, 1986). Assaults by strangers are more likely to evoke feelings of anxiety, increased startle response, and increased fear. Assaults by a known person are more likely to be associated with depression, guilt, and lowered self-concept.

The availability of a support group during the crisis period is important. Support groups can reduce the stigmatizing effects of victimization and provide a comparison point by which the student-victim may gauge her own reaction. However, fear of reporting the incident to a campus service (such as police) that may make a referral to the student counseling center, and hesitance to seek mental health services in general, may inhibit the counseling center's ability to form such groups. Networking may be an alternative. Connecting victim-survivors at some point, or having recovered victims serve as volunteers at student counseling centers, may be other ways to arrange mutual support.

The availability of on-campus services is paramount. The student counseling center should provide assessment and treatment services. Referral to off-campus agencies should be avoided. Sending a victimized student away from the campus gives a negative message—"we don't want you here"—an unintended message, perhaps, but still negative. Student counseling services should be ready to deal with the problems that students experience on the campus.

In situations of interpersonal violence, the involvement of student counseling services must be central. Student psychological services can intervene with the victim, train personnel in recognition and treatment (particularly of battering), train university police as interveners, and undertake community interventions with residence halls and other segments of the campus.

Victims of sexual assault and spousal abuse are increasingly recognized as needing psychological as well as medical intervention. While the institutional response to male-female violence has improved, services need continued improvement and expansion. Victims of other campus violence need services as well; male victims of physical assault related to alcohol use, racism, and homophobia are examples. Training campus personnel (security, health services, and so on) to enhance their sensitivity and responsiveness to all victim-survivors of violence will increase the likelihood that students are referred for needed counseling.

Prevention

The institutional response to violence can be conceptualized in two broad areas: prevention and intervention. With regard to prevention, educational programs and media can be developed to address interpersonal violence on a specific campus. An example might be a videotape about date rape, which could be presented in an arena likely to have high student participation (such as freshman orientation or fraternity and sorority rush week). Programs tailored to smaller specific audiences (say, occupants of a residence hall or a fraternity house) provide for follow-up and allow for more discussion. Follow-up later in the year strengthens the initial message and underscores the university administration's concern for students' safety.

An important issue to be included in preventive education programs on sexual assault is the substance abuse–sexual assault connection. Students can participate in discussions and role playing about how assaults and violence are escalated by drugs and alcohol. Discussions can take place both in drug awareness programs and in rape prevention programs.

Preventive education that focuses on nonaggressive behavior in interpersonal relationships is another important component. A male student needs to understand that when a woman says no, she means no, and that he must respect that message. Male students can be helped to explore their feelings about women's resistance to their advances and their attitudes about acceptable behavior in dating relationships. Female students can be helped to explore their feelings about saying no to sexual advances and their difficulties in negotiating in relationships.

When an assault has occurred, intervention is recommended. The assault of a friend, roommate, or classmate has a strong impact on others. This indirect victimization may result in heightened fear, mistrust, depression, and so on. For example, if a woman is raped in her residence hall, other residents are likely to be affected by the event, even though they did not experience the victimization directly. Providing support and acknowledging such reactions may reduce prolonged psychological effects and mobilize the resources of the group to deal with the traumatic event. Debriefing sessions should be held as soon as possible after the event, in the residence hall. If the event is dealt with in a group, the members are more likely to be resources for one another and for the victim than if student counseling personnel assume a more passive role and wait for persons especially distressed by the event to come in for services. Reactions can be put in a trauma framework, which serves to normalize the range of potential responses.

Obviously, such efforts need good working relations and cooperation between student counseling and health services, housing, and other administrative units. Good working relationships with student groups (sororities and fraternities, ethnic-identified organizations, and so on) prior to a traumatic event serve to ease access to specific groups and to limit the potential for conflict and misunderstanding around how response to the event is handled.

University administrators need to openly acknowledge violence and tensions (racial, and so on) as campus problems. Treating such issues as individual or special group problems is likely to perpetuate conflict. Gaining awareness of on-campus crime and victimization is an important first step on the part of administrators. A recent survey ("Many College Officials . . . ," 1989) found that many college officials are not well informed about assaults on their campuses.

Immediately making information about an event public may help the college community reach resolution. For example, UCLA releases a description and a composite sketch of the assailant, along with information about the assault, immediately after any rape reported as having occurred on campus. This bulletin serves to inform the campus, increase awareness, and, potentially, aid efforts to locate the assailant.

Preestablished policies—about media notification, reward or other compensation for information leading to the arrest of a perpetrator, contact with kin, and the release of crime-on-campus statistics—are among the many issues that are best addressed when the system is not in flux. It is best to make these decisions proactively, rather than in response to a specific incident. Colleges and universities probably will be under increased public scrutiny around these issues. To this end, a campuswide interdisciplinary committee on violence can establish policy recommendations for the university. Faculty and staff, student, and parent representation on this committee are equally important.

One issue of current concern, which needs the university administration's guidance, is the responsibility to warn. Helping the victim decide between legal prosecution and the institutional disciplinary system (in the case of a student-to-student assault) is an important intervention in the crisis. If a student-client chooses not to report an assault, confidentiality in the counseling setting should be respected. To inform institutional administrators of the victimization of a student, a mechanism should be developed so that the counseling center can notify administrators without identifying the victim. This action may also help to identify patterns of assault on campus and increase preventive action. Individual state laws may dictate specific action for therapists, and so legal statutes should be consulted.

Conclusion

Victims of crime and violence on college campuses are likely to benefit from specific services offered by the student counseling center. Individual crisis intervention and support groups can help the victim-survivor regain a sense of competence, reestablish a sense of continuity and meaning in life, and resume normal activities.

Response to victimization can be thought of as a normal reaction to an abnormal event. Recovery can be conceptualized as a series of potential crises, including the reactions of others and dealing with victimization-related events (such as interaction with police officers). Focusing intervention on victimization and recovery can restore a sense of mastery and reduce self-blame.

Interpersonal violence on college campuses has far-reaching consequences and is not an issue solely for criminal justice. University systems need to increase both awareness and cooperation to deal effectively with campus violence. This chapter has outlined an intervention approach and offered suggestions for both prevention and universitywide management of violent incidents.

Resources

Various educational videotapes are available—for example, *It Still Hurts,* by Auburn University (1985), and *Rethinking Rape,* by LePage (1985). Previewing of these and other videos is strongly encouraged as a way to determine which would be most appropriate for the target population.

Student counseling personnel should be aware of services available through victim/witness assistance programs. Many states have established such programs to provide assistance to victims and witnesses of certain crimes. Services include assessment and referral, compensation for costs incurred as a consequence of the crime (medical bills and psychotherapy bills are often included in this coverage), and court accompaniment, which is especially helpful for those not familiar with the court system and its proceedings. It may be helpful to coordinate services to meet a student's needs. Local district attorneys may be good sources of information about services offered on the local level.

Because training with victims of violence is rarely a part of graduate school curricula, student counseling personnel may want to expand their existing clinical skills to include treatment with victims of crime and violence. Training opportunities currently are expanding in this area. The National Organization for Victim Assistance (Washington, D.C.) is one of a number of agencies offering specialized training.

References

Aizenman, M., and Kelley, G. "The Incidence of Violence and Acquaintance Rape in Dating Relationships Among College Men and Women." *Journal of College Student Development*, 1988, *29*, 305–311.

Auburn University. *It Still Hurts.* (Videotape.) Goshen, Ky.: Campus Crime Prevention Programs, Auburn University, 1985.

Bard, M., and Sangrey, D. *The Crime Victim's Book.* (2nd ed.) New York: Brunner/Mazel, 1986.

Federal Bureau of Investigation. *Uniform Crime Reports: Crime in the United States.* Washington, D.C.: U.S. Government Printing Office, 1988.

Hirschorn, M. W. "A Parental Crusade to Force Colleges to Reveal Crime Data." *Chronicle of Higher Education*, September 2, 1987, p. A3.

Janoff-Bulman, R. "Characterological Versus Behavioral Self-Blame: Inquiries into Depression and Rape." *Journal of Personality and Social Psychology*, 1979, *37*, 1798–1809.

Kanin, E. J. "Male Aggression in Dating-Courting Relations." *American Journal of Sociology*, 1957, *63*, 197–204.

Kanin, E. J., and Parcell, S. R. "Sexual Aggression: A Second Look at the Offended Female." *Archives of Sexual Behavior*, 1977, *6*, 67–76.

Katz, B. L., and Burt, M. R. "Effects of Familiarity with the Rapist on Post-Rape Recovery." Paper presented at the meeting of the American Psychological Association, Washington, D. C., August 1986.

Katz, B. L., and Burt, M. R. "Self-Blame in Recovery from Rape: Help or Hindrance?" In A. W. Burgess (ed.), *Rape and Sexual Assault II.* New York: Garland Publishing, 1988.

Kirkpatrick, C., and Kanin, E. "Male Sex Aggression on a University Campus." *American Sociological Revolution*, 1957, *22*, 52–58.

Koss, M. P. "The Hidden Rape Victim: Personality, Attitudinal, and Situational Characteristics." *Psychology of Women Quarterly*, 1985, *9*, 193–212.

Koss, M. P., Gidycz, C. A., and Wisniewski, N. "The Scope of Rape: Incidence and Prevalence of Sexual Aggression and Victimization in a National Sample of Higher Education Students." *Journal of Consulting and Clinical Psychology*, 1987, *55*, 162–170.

Koss, M. P., Leonard, K. E., Beezley, D. A., and Oros, C. J. "Nonstranger Sexual Aggression: A Discriminant Analysis of the Psychological Characteristics of Undetected Offenders." *Sex Roles*, 1985, *12*, 981–992.

Koss, M. P., and Oros, C. J. "Sexual Experiences Survey: A Research Instrument Investigating Sexual Aggression and Victimization." *Journal of Consulting and Clinical Psychology*, 1982, *50*, 455–457.

LePage, J. *Rethinking Rape.* (Videotape.) Palo Alto, Calif.: Stanford University, 1985.

Levy, B., and Brown, V. B. "Strategies for Crisis Intervention with Victims of

Violence." In S. Saunders, A. M. Anderson, C. A. Hart, and G. M. Rubenstein (eds.), *Violent Individuals and Families*. Springfield, Ill.: Thomas, 1984.

McCann, I. L., Sakheim, D. K., and Abrahamson, D. J. "Trauma and Victimization: A Model of Psychological Adaptation." *Counseling Psychologist*, 1988, *16*, 531–594.

Malamuth, N. M. "Rape Proclivity Among Males." *Journal of Social Issues*, 1981, *37*, 138–157.

"Many College Officials Are Found to Be Ignorant of Crime on Their Campuses." *Chronicle of Higher Education*, January 25, 1989, pp. A31–A32.

"Mass Protest." *Time*, February 29, 1988, p. 96.

Muehlenhard, C. L., and Linton, M. A. "Date Rape and Sexual Aggression in Dating Situations: Incidence and Risk Factors." *Journal of Counseling Psychology*, 1987, *34*, 186–196.

O'Leary, K. D., and Arias, I. "Prevalence, Correlates, and Development of Spouse Abuse." In R. DeV. Peters and R. J. McMahon (eds.), *Social Learning and Systems Approaches to Marriage and the Family*. New York: Brunner/Mazel, 1988.

Rapaport, K., and Burkhart, B. R. "Personality and Attitudinal Characteristics of Sexually Coercive Males." *Journal of Abnormal Psychology*, 1984, *93*, 216–221.

Rouse, L. P. "Abuse in Dating Relationships: A Comparison of Blacks, Whites, and Hispanics." *Journal of College Student Development*, 1988, *29*, 312–319.

Salasin, S. A. "Services to Victims: Needs Assessment." In S. A. Salasin (ed.), *Evaluating Victim Services*. Newbury Park, Calif.: Sage, 1981.

Sherrill, J. M., and Siegel, D. G. (eds.). *Responding to Violence on Campus*. New Directions for Student Services, no. 47. San Francisco: Jossey-Bass, 1989.

Sorenson, S. B., and Golding, J. M. "Depressive Concomitants of Recent Criminal Victimization." *Journal of Traumatic Stress*, in press.

Symonds, M. "The Second Injury to Victims of Violent Crime." *Evaluation and Change*, Spring 1980, pp. 36–38.

Susan B. Sorenson is an assistant research epidemiologist and lecturer in the School of Public Health at the University of California, Los Angeles. A licensed clinical psychologist, she has published research on sexual assault, suicide, homicide, crime victims, and family violence.

Vivian B. Brown is chief executive officer of PROTOTYPES, a center for innovation in health, mental health, and social services. She is also a consultant for student psychological services at the University of California, Los Angeles, and for substance abuse prevention at the California Institute of Technology.

AIDS is the ultimate crisis of the 1980s and 1990s.

The AIDS Crisis:
Intervention and Prevention

Vivian B. Brown

AIDS (acquired immunodeficiency syndrome) is our most dramatic crisis. It highlights all of the problems that have plagued our society for many years—namely, drug abuse, prostitution, poor health care for those unable to pay, homophobia, racism, sexism, and so on. Although there have not been a dramatic number of cases of AIDS reported among college and university students at this time, our students are at risk on the basis of a number of their behaviors, and there may be students who are asymptomatically infected but can transmit HIV (human immunodeficiency virus) to others. Given the long incubation period, a student engaged in high-risk behaviors may not show recognizable AIDS symptoms until he or she has left college. High-risk behaviors for students include selection of multiple sexual partners, experimentation with a number of sexual activities without latex protection, and experimentation with drugs (including intravenous drugs). The most important goals for colleges and institutions are increasing awareness and providing education to prevent further spread of AIDS, and providing sensitive and informed crisis intervention.

If we are to provide a full range of AIDS services, including crisis intervention and prevention, it is important to understand the progresion of AIDS and psychosocial responses at each stage. AIDS represents the ultimate stage of the crisis matrix (see Chapter One), beginning with the first symptoms or with a diagnosis of HIV seropositivity (the detection of HIV antibodies in the blood). The crisis matrix defines a period, extending over several months to several years, during which the individual is likely to experience a series of crises. Morin and Batchelor (1984), Nichols

(1985), and Tross and Hirsch (1988) have utilized a crisis model for psychosocial reactions and AIDS interventions. However, they have not utilized more recent thinking about the concept of the crisis matrix. Table 1 illustrates the different crisis points along the crisis matrix, including events, the meaning of the events, coping strategies, and possible outcomes. Table 1 shows a number of crisis points and scenarios, to demonstrate the process of moving through the crisis matrix and to show the complexity possible within the AIDS crisis matrix. It is not meant as a simple step-by-step guide. What we do not want to forget is that there is a person moving through this period of time. The course of illness may vary, and therefore the sequence of events will vary. The meanings will vary with each individual. Coping begins with the individual's usual strategies and then moves more toward coping with a terminal illness (while, hopefully, maintaining hope).

Table 1. AIDS Crisis Matrix

Event	Meaning	Coping	Outcome
First symptoms (or lover has AIDS)	I have AIDS; I will die; I am sick	Denial, anxiety; getting information	Ignoring, numbing; seeing physician, getting tested
Positive HIV test	I have AIDS; I will lose everyone; I am dirty	Anxiety, depression; substance use	Numbing; suicide attempt
Diagnosis of ARC/AIDS	I am dying	Anxiety, depression, preoccupation with illness	Withdrawal
Telling family	I am punished; they know now that I am a _____	Seeking support	Increased support; rejection
Rejection by family	I am unloved, unworthy	Suicide attempt	Crisis intervention
Treatment (AZT)	I will not die	Improved diet; no substances; meditation	Improved health
Return of infections	I am dying	Increased efforts; anxiety	Suicidal ideation
Remission	I am a survivor	Anxiety, hypervigilance	Opportunity to make plans/final wishes
AIDS dementia		Anxiety; anger	Acceptance of limitations

Intervention Through the Course of Illness

First Symptoms. Studies of life-threatening illnesses (Hackett and Cassem, 1970; Horowitz, 1973) have shown that the initial response is often denial, alternating with periods of overwhelming anxiety. Denial may be so strong that the individual does not seek further medical services or HIV testing. A student at this stage may be so overwhelmed by anxiety that he or she may not retain information at all or may distort what is said. If a student's lover has received a diagnosis of AIDS or ARC (AIDS-related complex), similar responses may be seen.

Intervention at this point involves reducing the anxiety and assessing the extent of the denial. If the student is following up with medical checkups or HIV testing, the denial should be seen as a normal response to the crisis and should not be challenged. The student needs to feel supported by the crisis intervener, so that he or she will disclose additional information about risky behavior.

Pretest HIV counseling is extremely important for students at this initial stage. Studies are reporting that there may be gains in risk reduction as a result of HIV testing in seropositive persons, but there is also the possibility of serious emotional consequences (Frigo and others, 1986). There are also some reports that individuals who receive negative HIV test results may maintain risky behavior.

Confidentiality with regard to HIV testing is a complex issue. Students need to understand the differences between anonymous and confidential testing. Counselors should consult state reporting requirements and inform students of any confidentiality limitations before testing occurs.

Positive HIV Test. Posttest counseling must be extremely sensitive and crisis-oriented. If the student has tested positive for HIV antibodies, anxiety and depression may again become overwhelming. The counselor's task is to reduce the anxiety, give accurate information, allow ventilation of feelings, and explore further actions. If the student has used drugs or alcohol, it is important that such use be discussed and that the student be encouraged to abstain. A follow-up session should always be scheduled.

If the student has tested negative, it is extremely important to explore the meanings of a negative HIV test and to reinforce accurate information regarding reduction of risky behavior. A follow-up test should also be scheduled. In either case (positive or negative test), the mandate to maintain safer sex and abstain from drugs may precipitate another crisis point and should therefore be discussed with the student.

Diagnosis of AIDS or ARC. The impacts of being diagnosed with a life-threatening illness have been characterized as preoccupation with mortality, a sense of personal vulnerability, and heightened emotional distress (Weisman and Worden, 1976). Studies have shown that men with a diagnosis of ARC scored as high as and sometimes higher than those with AIDS on multiple measures of distress (Tross and others, 1986; Temoshok, 1986). Uncertainty about developing AIDS may put these men at even greater risk for emotional distress.

Crisis intervention at this point on the crisis matrix focuses on anxiety, depression, and preoccupation with illness. The counselor may receive numerous telephone calls and requests for information from the student. Suicidal ideation should be explored, particularly in students who have made previous suicide attempts, have watched close friends or lovers die of AIDS, or have histories of serious substance abuse.

Telling the Family. While telling family members about a diagnosis of AIDS or HIV seropositivity may bring increased support, it is also possible that a family may be hearing about a student's homosexuality, drug use, or multiple sex partners for the first time. This increases the likelihood of negative response on the part of family members and may lead to rejection of the student. If at all possible, this step should be explored with the student before he or she tells family members. In this way, additional stress may be avoided or postponed.

Similar issues arise with regard to telling a sexual partner or spouse. In this case, however, it is important for the student to consider informing the partner, who will be at high risk and will need to make informed decisions. Students may wish to enlist the assistance of the counselor to inform spouses or sexual partners.

Rejection by Family. For some students, the crisis that brings them into the counseling center may be loss of family support. Faced with other losses—of an image of the self as healthy or invulnerable, or of specific risky sexual or drug-use behaviors—the student may see loss of family support as the last straw. In addition to assisting the student in understanding all the losses he or she has experienced, the counselor needs to allow for ventilation of feelings and to begin the exploration of new social supports. At this stage, it is important to have groups available. These may include an HIV-positive support group and AIDS support groups.

Treatment. As new drugs are found to be effective (for example, AZT), changes in the course of AIDS will be seen. It is important for the crisis intervener to explore the meaning of the treatment for the particular student and to assist in exploring future actions that will maintain the lowest-risk behavior. If the student experiences the return of infections or other symptoms, there will again be downward movement; if the student experiences remission, there will be renewed hope. The crisis intervener's task is to help the student balance between preparing for death and sustaining hope.

AIDS Dementia. The AIDS dementia complex is characterized by global cognitive deterioration; in the early stages, it is marked by mental slowing and deficits in recent memory. Patients with AIDS dementia often are aware of their neurological symptoms and respond with anxiety, depression, and anger. The major tasks of the crisis intervener are to assess cognitive deficits, refer the client for regular monitoring by a neurologist, and assist the client in accepting the limitations on cognitive ability.

Prevention

Education is of primary importance in preventing the further spread of AIDS. Many colleges and universities have already established ongoing AIDS preventive education programs on their campuses. Health educators representing university AIDS prevention programs have said that they are now looking for the answers to a "second generation" of questions (Biemiller, 1987). The following sections highlight some important second-generation issues and concepts related to AIDS prevention.

Health-Belief Model. Most campus AIDS education programs are based on the health-belief model, which postulates that individuals will change their behavior if they perceive themselves to be potentially at risk, believe that the recommended new behavior will be effective in reducing risk, and anticipate few difficulties in undertaking the recommended actions. In AIDS prevention with college students, there are difficulties with each of these points.

Few college students believe that they are at risk for AIDS. It is difficult for them to believe they are at risk if they are not intravenous drug users or homosexual. In part, this is denial of any vulnerability, but it is also a response to confused and confusing messages about risks. There have been articles written stating that heterosexuals who do not use drugs are not at risk. There has been a focus on at-risk groups, rather than on risky behavior. In addition, many people, including college students, do not anticipate "few difficulties" with regard to using condoms. While the message is clear to use condoms, we seem to deny that many people do not use them all the time. It is also true that students know that condoms have not proved 100 percent effective. There are many obstacles to condom utilization, and we need to address them and teach students negotiation skills. The obstacles include students' lack of knowledge about using condoms effectively, awkwardness in discussing condom use with partners, unwillingness to "break the mood," unwillingness to question or be questioned about prior sexual partners and practices, and the belief that condoms reduce enjoyment. All of these issues need to be addressed in preventive education.

Peer Support. As mentioned, the health-belief model has been the basis for most of the AIDS education programs implemented on campus. Another factor, in addition to the three already shown as related to health-improving behavior, is the knowledge that one's peers are undertaking recommended actions. It is important for college students to hear from their peers that they are using risk-reduction behavior (using condoms, not using drugs). Peer education programs can be the most effective ones for getting the message out across campuses. Intensive personal communications also need to be an integral part of prevention programming on campus; educational workshops will not be sufficient to effect behavior change.

Culturally Sensitive Education and Materials. Besides using peers to get the message out, it is extremely important that we design our programs to fit the diverse student populations on our campuses. The following points should be considered:

1. It is important to use language that is culturally sensitive to each population. Educational workshops and materials should be in the languages of the students who participate, and the use of certain words to describe behaviors should be culturally relevant.

2. Issues of racism, sexism, and homophobia need to be addressed in every educational program. With regard to awareness of racial and ethnic minority issues, it is important to recognize some of the myths and beliefs in the communities ("The white medical establishment is trying to infect ethnic minority populations"; "HIV testing will give you AIDS"). While many college students have accurate knowledge regarding AIDS, discussion of these myths and beliefs may still be important.

3. Many of the materials being disseminated are not designed for the diverse college populations. It is important to have college students design materials (writings and videotapes) for other college students. There are many talented students who are studying a multitude of subjects; they could be enlisted to design curricula related to their major fields of study. For example, theater arts students could write plays dealing with AIDS; journalism majors could write articles for college newspapers to get out the latest information; medical and nursing students, and psychology and social work majors, could design training programs on AIDS for their respective disciplines, as well as for interdisciplinary teams; and business majors could address the issue of AIDS and the workplace, drafting policies for corporations.

Women and AIDS. Women have been called a hidden at-risk population. A woman student may not know that she is at risk because she may not know that her male sexual partner has had sex with HIV-positive individuals or shared intravenous needles. Women students who are in lesbian relationships may believe that they are not at risk at all, and they may not question whether their partners have had sex with HIV-positive men or shared needles. Attention has turned recently toward women, and prevention programs are designed to address their special needs.

In most preventive education programs for women, a core theme is empowerment. As part of AIDS prevention for women students, it is important to discuss issues of self-esteem and power. Women also need to learn how to negotiate with their sexual partners to persuade them to practice safer sex.

In a recent workshop on the development of an AIDS prevention model for female sexual partners of intravenous drug users, eight primary issues were identified for the women: dependency in relationships; sexuality; contraception and pregnancy; health; sexually transmitted diseases; addictions; domestic violence; and death, dying, and loss.

The AIDS Network. The AIDS network—agencies and staff involved in AIDS prevention and intervention—is growing every day. Counseling center staff can call on colleagues off campus to provide additional human and materials resources. The explosion of information regarding AIDS makes it almost impossible to keep up with the latest research, materials, and programs. Many staff involved with AIDS work will be happy to share their resources and consult on designing new programs.

Conclusion

AIDS is our most dramatic crisis. It is a life-threatening syndrome with no known cure. In many instances, AIDS is fatal. The most important goals for institutions are to increase awareness and provide education aimed at preventing further spread of AIDS and to provide sensitive and informed crisis intervention services.

In order to provide a full range of services, institutions need to understand the progression of AIDS and psychosocial responses at each stage. The AIDS crisis matrix begins with the first symptoms, or with a diagnosis of HIV seropositivity, and may extend through AIDS dementia to death.

References

Biemiller, L. "A 'Second Generation' of Questions Hits AIDS Education Programs." *Chronicle of Higher Education,* July 1, 1987, pp. 21–22.

Frigo, M. A., Zones, J. S., Beeson, D. R., Rutherford, G. W., Echenberg, D. F., and O'Malley, P. M. "The Impact of Structured Counseling in Acute Adverse Psychiatric Reactions Associated with LAV/HTLV-III Antibody Testing." Abstract 284. Paper presented at the 114th annual meeting of the American Public Health Association, Las Vegas, Nevada, 1986.

Hackett, T. P., and Cassem, N. H. "Psychological Reactions to a Life-Threatening Illness." In H. Abram (ed.), *Psychological Aspects of Stress.* Springfield, Ill.: Thomas, 1970.

Horowitz, M. T. *Stress Response Syndromes.* Northvale, N.J.: Aronson, 1973.

Morin, S. F., and Batchelor, W. F. "Responding to the Psychological Crisis of AIDS." *Public Health Reports,* 1984, *99,* 4–9.

Nichols, S. E. "Psychosocial Reactions of Persons with the Acquired Immunodeficiency Syndrome." *Annals of Internal Medicine,* 1985, *103,* 765–767.

Temoshok, L. "Psychosocial Coping with a Diagnosis of AIDS." Paper presented at the annual meeting of the Society of Behavioral Medicine, San Francisco, 1986.

Tross, S., and Hirsch, D. A. "Psychological Distress and Neuropsychological Complications of HIV Infection and AIDS." *American Psychologist,* 1988, *43,* 929–934.

Tross, S., Holland, J., Hirsch, D. A., Schiffman, M., Gold, J., and Safai, B. "Psychological and Social Impact of AIDS Spectrum Disorders." In *Proceedings of the Second International Conference on Acquired Immunodeficiency Syndrome.* Paris: Voyage Conseil, 1986.

Weisman, A., and Worden, W. "The Existential Plight in Cancer: Significance of the First 100 Days." *International Journal of Psychiatry and Medicine,* 1976, *7,* 1–15.

Vivian B. Brown is chief executive officer of PROTOTYPES, a center for innovation in health, mental health, and social services. She is also a consultant for student psychological services at the University of California, Los Angeles; a consultant for substance abuse prevention at the California Institute of Technology; and deputy principal investigator of the Women and AIDS Risk Network (WARN Project).

Future directions for counseling centers and selected references for center staff are presented.

Present and Future Issues

Harold L. Pruett, Vivian B. Brown

Implementation of a crisis program can be difficult and frustrating. Counseling center staff are often reluctant to follow through with crisis intervention unless there is ample opportunity for training and support. Crisis intervention is also an active approach, requiring hard, focused work, and many therapists see it as a second-best approach. It is probably most effective when specific staff members—a core group of interveners—are selected, who are willing to learn a new model and who view short-term approaches as positive alternatives.

While the theory of crisis may seem simplistic, individual crisis intervention is in fact a very complicated model to understand and requires considerable skill to use properly. It is often difficult for professional staff to understand this complexity and use proper techniques. The crisis model described in Chapter One allows for complex dynamic formulations and allows counseling staff with different theoretical orientations to speak a common language.

Aside from consideration of staff issues, it is important to have alternative modalities for students who require extended intervention that goes beyond the initial six sessions. A group therapy component is an ideal follow-up modality for students who require ongoing work. Groups provide students with an excellent "living laboratory" in which to learn new interpersonal skills and practice new behaviors.

Rapid entry into a crisis program is also absolutely essential. Students should not have to wait more than three or four days from the date that they first contact the center for an initial appointment. Clients should then be informed that they will be seen for up to six sessions, but that many people are helped in even less time. A clear policy needs to be established—that if the student needs further help after crisis intervention, the crisis therapist will not see him or her. Strict adherence to the crisis model is essential to maximizing results.

Training

In our opinion, training of staff on core crisis work is essential. Too often, staff are trained in traditional approaches to intervention, which often translate into individual ongoing therapy and counseling. A short-term problem-solving focus is often lacking. Some staff have also been trained according to a problem-solving orientation, without a psychodynamic perspective. Crisis intervention offers both—a short-term problem-solving orientation and a psychodynamic perspective. In addition, the concepts of community intervention and prevention are often unfamiliar, and staff are often uncomfortable working outside their offices and on the campus. Crisis intervention extends the intervention work to larger and larger audiences.

The concepts described in Chapter One are the basic ones necessary for staff training. Staff members need to understand the model and its key concepts. We have utilized role playing and videotapes to demonstrate how the first session could look. Staff members need an opportunity to try out the model. We have found that it is important for staff to be open and honest about their attitudes and feelings at the outset of training, and then to be open about reporting their first experiences with trying the model.

Some of the problems that staff have encountered are (1) difficulty in maintaining a crisis focus and resisting the temptation to move into the "rich," long-term material that the student may present, (2) difficulty in finding a crisis with some students, (3) problems with the type of therapeutic relationship in the crisis model, (4) issues of aftercare, (5) problems with crisis versus brief therapy models, and (6) their own needs (for example, the desire to do a number of hours of extended therapy).

Another important area to address after training is ongoing supervision and consultation. In our experience, it is necessary to have experienced crisis interveners available to the staff, in order to continue training and technical assistance. Some problems have been encountered by professionals moving into supervising the crisis model. For example, supervision needs to be more active. There may also be an inability to supervise crisis cases when one has not had many years of experience. It may be difficult to distinguish diagnostic categories or find a crisis, or students may have waited two weeks to be seen and may no longer be in crisis.

The Future

If a recent report (Astin and others, 1988) accurately predicts how future students will experience colleges and universities, counseling centers will find themselves dealing with increasing numbers of students who show increasing signs of disturbance. This study found that 10.5 percent of entering freshmen in the fall of 1988 reported feeling depressed frequently, and 21.5 percent reported feeling overwhelmed. These figures are the highest ever reported in the twenty-three years that the survey has been conducted. According to Astin and others (1988, p. 9), "Taken together, various items from the 1988 survey point to rising stress among college freshmen. The increase in smoking, coupled with the rising numbers of students feeling depressed, feeling overwhelmed, and the decline in self-assessed emotional health, are all indicators of rising stress levels among students."

The trend over the past two or three years has certainly been for counseling centers to see more students who had psychiatric histories before entering college. In a 1987 nationwide survey of counseling centers, the number of students hospitalized for psychological reasons was reported to have increased by 17 percent from the year before (Gallagher, 1987).

Offer and Spiro (1987) undertook an epidemiological study of high school students and followed a sample of them into college; 20 percent of these students were considered disturbed and in need of mental health care: "It seems to us that because so many disturbed adolescents go to college (20 percent), and since half of college dropouts do so for a variety of mental health reasons, it behooves us to pay more attention to this problem than we have in the past" (Offer and Spiro, 1987, p. 214).

The campus community will find itself increasingly involved with many issues, aside from the purely developmental ones. The crises of substance abuse and AIDS that have rocked this country are examples of issues that require addressing. Campus communities are not immune to these concerns and will require assistance from personnel in student affairs. The counseling center will have to involve itself more in community intervention if it is to remain vital in the years ahead. While campus administrators will be more in need of the expertise available in the campus counseling and mental health centers, those centers will also need to prove their worth.

With forecasts of increasing pathology, increasing problems with substance abuse, and continued high competition, there will probably be more crises occurring in the next several years. These things are somewhat predictable. We know that the demand for services will not keep up with resources. Our experience with the AIDS crisis, however, tells us that there are some things that we cannot predict with any accuracy. These kinds of crises mean that the centers have to be prepared to be flexible and move quickly when a new hazard arises that affects the campus community. The counseling center must take an active role in dealing with these new crises. In addition, counseling center staff are likely to be more knowledgeable about crisis and community intervention than people are in student affairs.

Updating the Counseling Center

For the counseling center to remain on top of the changes in student and campus issues and be responsive to the community, the centers should have a plan that includes the following elements:

1. There should be annual monitoring of presenting problems and needs assessment, to pick up new trends.

2. Staffing needs to be diverse, so that a range of skills will be available, as well as staff members of varying ethnicity, gender, and so on.

3. Self-help programs and peer programs are worth considering. Some may dispute their worth, but we have always found peer counseling programs and self-help programs to be an important adjunct to the work of the counseling center. Such programs can free staff to do other kinds of work that require greater expertise and can also provide the center with helpful feedback regarding student issues on the campus. Peer counselors can be trained in generic crisis work, such as work with students who have experienced the breakup of a relationship or who need an AIDS support group.

4. Services can be expanded to family members by means of a family crisis intervention model. Often the counseling center does not or cannot offer services to family members. In our opinion, it may be important to consider this modality, partly because it may also be a source of revenue for the counseling center.

5. There should be increased emphasis on consultation to faculty and staff. Students are not the only members of the community who experience crises. At times, what first appears as a student's crisis may in fact be a crisis of a staff member or faculty member.

6. There should be increased emphasis on prevention programming, with specific time allocations in staff members' schedules. Under the pressure of direct service demands, prevention activities are often the first to go.

Annotated Bibliography

This sourcebook is intended as a practical guide, derived from our own experiences and those of our colleagues. The following sources of additional information have been selected because we believe they will provide a range of reference material and resources relevant to the topics we have presented.

Adams, A., and Abarbanel, G. *Sexual Assault on Campus: What Colleges Can Do.* Santa Monica, Calif.: Santa Monica Hospital Medical Center, 1988.

This guide targets university administrators, outlining recommendations for sexual assault policies, procedures, and programs on campus.

Aguilera, D. C., and Messick, J. M. *Crisis Intervention: Theory and Methodology.* St. Louis: Mosby, 1986.

This is a very practical book on various crises and includes four topics on intervention. It is easy to read and offers many good case examples.

Backer, T. E., Batchelor, W. F., Jones, J. M., and Mays, V. M. "Special Issue: Psychology and AIDS." *American Psychologist*, 1988, *43*, entire issue.

This special issue covers many important topics regarding AIDS, including prevention, intervention, and scientific information.

Bloom, B. L. *Community Mental Health: A General Introduction.* Monterey, Calif.: Brooks/Cole, 1984.

This book presents an excellent overview of community mental health, ranging from brief therapy and crisis intervention to prevention programs.

Brown, S. *Treating the Alcoholic: A Developmental Model of Recovery.* New York: Wiley, 1985.

This is an excellent overview of the problem of alcohol. It features descriptions of interventions, including AA and other twelve-step approaches.

Drye, R. C., Goulding, R. L., and Goulding, M. E. "No-Suicide Decisions: Patient Monitoring of Suicidal Risk." *American Journal of Psychiatry*, 1973, *130*, 171–174.

This article is an excellent resource for discussing no-suicide contracts and presents a rationale for evaluating and working with suicidal clients. It is strongly recommended for all staff.

Jacobson, G. F. (ed.). *Crisis Intervention in the 1980s.* New Directions for Mental Health Services, no. 6. San Francisco: Jossey-Bass, 1980.

This volume presents an up-to-date overview of crisis intervention with individuals, families, and communities. An excellent theoretical presentation of individual crisis intervention is provided, which can be very helpful in orienting staff to the complexities of this approach.

Johnston, L. D., O'Malley, P. M., and Bachman, J. G. *National Trends in Drug Use and Related Factors Among American High School Students and Young Adults, 1975–1986.* Rockville, Md.: National Institute of Drug Abuse, 1987.
This study shows statistical trends in drug use among young adults. (The same group of researchers publishes the annual "Monitoring the Future" reports.)

Kahn, A. (ed.). *Final Report: American Psychological Association Task Force on the Victims of Crime and Violence.* Washington, D.C.: American Psychological Association, 1984.
Although this report is not specifically targeted at college violence, student counseling personnel may find it helpful.

Keeling, R. P. *AIDS on the College Campus: ACHA Special Report.* Rockville, Md.: American College Health Association, 1986.
This is an excellent report about AIDS on campus, covering many important recomendations. It should be required reading for any student services professional.

Schneidman, E. *Definition of Suicide.* New York: Wiley, 1985.
This book, by a world-renowned thanatologist, presents some very important insights into suicide. It should be required reading for staff who deal with suicidal clients. It does not offer too much in the way of practical advice, but it features excellent conceptualization.

Walker, L. *The Battered Woman.* New York: Harper & Row, 1979.
This book is a classic on the subject of physical violence in intimate relationships.

Warshaw, R. *I Never Called It Rape.* New York: Harper & Row, 1988.
This is an easy-to-read book on date and acquaintance rape. It lists books, pamphlets, posters, videos, films, and program guides that may be of help in developing campus interventions.

Other Resources

Alcohol and Drug Abuse Clearing House, 444 No. Capitol, N.W., Suite 181, Washington, D.C. 20001.

This agency disseminates information about prevention programs for drugs, alcohol, and AIDS.

National Coalition Against Domestic Violence toll-free hotline: (202) 293-8860.

Dialing the toll-free number connects the caller with trained staff and volunteers, who provide information on domestic violence and shelters.

References

Astin, A. W., Green, K. C., Korn, W. S., Schalit, M., and Berz, E. R. *The American Freshman: National Norms for Fall 1988.* Los Angeles: Higher Education Research Institute, University of California, 1988.

Gallagher, R. P. *Counseling Center Survey and Directory, 1987.* Pittsburgh, Pa.: Counseling and Student Development Center, University of Pittsburgh, 1987.

Offer, D., and Spiro, R. P. "The Disturbed Adolescent Goes to College." *Journal of the American College Health Association,* 1987, *35,* 209–214.

Harold L. Pruett, director of student psychological services at the University of California, Los Angeles, is also chair of the Organization of Counseling Center Directors in Higher Education in California and past president and fellow of the Los Angeles Society of Clinical Psychologists.

Vivian B. Brown is chief executive officer of PROTOTYPES, a center for innovation in health, mental health, and social services. She is also a consultant for student psychological services at the University of California, Los Angeles, and for substance abuse prevention at the California Institute of Technology.

INDEX

Ordering Information

New Directions for Student Services is a series of paperback books that offers guidelines and programs for aiding students in their total development—emotional, social, and physical, as well as intellectual. Books in the series are published quarterly in Fall, Winter, Spring, and Summer and are available for purchase by subscription as well as by single copy.

Subscriptions for 1990 cost $42.00 for individuals (a savings of 20 percent over single-copy prices) and $56.00 for institutions, agencies, and libraries. Please do not send institutional checks for personal subscriptions. Standing orders are accepted.

Single copies cost $12.95 when payment accompanies order. (California, New Jersey, New York, and Washington, D.C., residents please include appropriate sales tax.) Billed orders will be charged postage and handling.

Discounts for quantity orders are available. Please write to the address below for information.

All orders must include either the name of an individual or an official purchase order number. Please submit your order as follows:
   Subscriptions: specify series and year subscription is to begin
   Single copies: include individual title code (such as SS1)

Mail all orders to:
   Jossey-Bass Inc., Publishers
   350 Sansome Street
   San Francisco, California 94104

DATE DUE

~~OCT 0 0 2007~~			
~~IN 137419~~			